ENGLAND
my
ENGLAND

A treasury of all things English

Tower of London, River Thames, London   Graham Byfield

Compiled by
GERRY HANSON

ROBSON BOOKS

First published in the United Kingdom in 2005 by
Robson Books
10 Southcombe Street
London
W14 0RA

An imprint of Anova Books Company Ltd

ISBN 9781861058935

A CIP catalogue record for this book is available from the British
Library.

10 9 8 7 6

Printed and bound by Creative Print and Design, Ebbw Vale, Wales

This book can be ordered direct from the publisher.
Contact the marketing department, but try your bookshop first.

www.anovabooks.com

*For Jill, whose extreme tolerance during the gestation
period of this book went above and beyond
the call of marital duty*

anthology /an-tho'lə-ji/ *n* a choice collection of writings, (esp poems), songs or paintings, etc; literally, a flower-gathering. [Gr, a collection of epigrams, literally, a flower-gathering, from *anthos* flower, and *-logia* gathering (from *leigein* to collect)]

*Chambers Dictionary,
New Ninth Edition*, 2003

St. George's Day Club

Founders: J C Byrne • E K Cornes MC • M H J Hornby

President: Air Vice-Marshal G C LAMB
CB CBE AFC RAF (Ret'd)

There is a forgotten, nay almost a forbidden word, which means more to me than any other: the word is "ENGLAND". Once we flaunted it in the face of the whole world like a banner. It was a word of power. But today we are scarcely allowed to mention the name of our Country.

I want to revive the grand old name of Englishman!

Sir Winston Churchill
KG, OMCH, TD

Contents

Foreword
The President of the St George's Day Club
Air Vice-Marshall 'Larry' Lamb CB, CBE, AFC,
RAF (Ret'd)

Ironically, the founding of the St George's Day Club owes not a little to foreign influence – Welsh to be precise – for it was on 1 March 1977 (St David's Day), that three friends met in a private house and made odious comparisons between the emotional Welsh and Irish celebrations of their patron saints and the phlegmatic indifference of the majority of Englishmen towards St George. Over what one of those present admits was more than 'a few' drinks, it was vowed among the three to redress the balance by endeavouring to form a St George's Day Club. Within a few days, a small band of like-minded patriots decided to have an informal lunch at the Busy Bee Restaurant on the Watford by-pass on the next St George's Day to assess the feasibility of forming such an organisation, which would be dedicated to upholding England and everything it stands for, and to ensure that in future, St George's Day would be properly celebrated.

'From little acorns, do mighty oak trees grow'. I suspect that even in their wildest dreams Eric Cornes, his co-founders, and the twenty or so friends who joined them at the Busy Bee never imagined the enthusiasm with which their decision to form the St George's Day Club would be greeted. After all, as small boys they had grown up in an era when the realms of the last King-Emperor, George VI, exceeded those of his great grand-mother Queen Victoria. As young men they had all lived through the rigours of the Second World War and, as they entered middle age, they were to witness that 500-year-old Empire, on which the sun never set, pass into the history books as the subjects of the Crown took over the reins of power to govern themselves. Yet whatever reservations might have been harboured over the darker side of Empire-building, the process had left a legacy of which they, and we, could be very proud. The cornerstone of that legacy, undoubtedly, has been the English language – the language of Chaucer, Milton, Shakespeare, Kipling and Churchill. An imperishable legacy – and it is entirely appropriate that one of today's Club members, Gerry Hanson, has devoted so much time and effort to collating some of the English language's more memorable quotations.

I commend this book to all who share the ideals that lie at the heart of the St George's Day Club and its members. I am sure its readers, as they browse through its pages, will gain both pleasure and inspiration from Gerry's selections.

'Larry' Lamb
2005

Introduction

In the preface to his book of essays, the sixteenth-century philosopher and essayist Michel Montaigne wrote: 'I have made a posie of other men's flowers, and only the thread that binds them is mine own.' Anyone who has read those essays will agree that Montaigne was being overly modest. However, his comment is a fairly accurate description of most anthologies – and this one is no exception.

Richard Ingrams, introducing his excellent 1989 *English Anthology*, makes the point that it has all been done before – and so it has. But because the selection of material is such a subjective process, every anthology differs. Mr Ingrams eschews sentimentality and flag-waving, and his book is a more academic work than mine. I am not averse to heart-tugging sentiment and am an unrepentant flag-waver. Thus I have included all the usual suspects – the much-loved favourites, the half-remembered verses – but there are contributions that I believe will be new to many readers. Furthermore, the wide-ranging selection goes beyond the conventional anthology to include articles, speeches and other items, ranging from the profound to the trivial, which gives an extra dimension to our view of England.

An anthology should inspire, amuse, delight and surprise in equal measure. But above all, an anthology about England should engender a spirit of pride in every true-born English man and woman, even at the risk of evoking envy in those not privileged to have been born in this great land. We English are not always comfortable with patriotism, unlike the Celtic fringes of the United Kingdom (the lands Michael Flanders refers to as 'the rottenmost parts of these islands of ours'). The Scots, Welsh and Irish have no inhibitions about extolling the virtues of their countries in prose, poetry and song, though they sometimes veer towards nationalism. Nationalism can, and often does, have ugly connotations, but patriotism, defined as 'love of one's country and a willingness to defend its freedom', is a noble concept. We owe it to all those who in the past have willingly defended its freedom to honour the land that gave us birth.

If this book persuades you of how fortunate you are to belong to what Ogden Nash once described as 'the most exclusive club on earth', I shall be extremely gruntled. And if you are English born, or of English stock but living overseas, I hope *England, My England* will remind you of why you can be proud of your English connections.

Cry 'God for Elizabeth, England and St George!'

Gerry Hanson
2005

There'll Always Be An England

If England was what England seems,
An' not the England of our dreams,
But only putty, brass, an' paint,
'Ow quick we'd drop 'er! But she ain't!

R u d y a r d   K i p l i n g

To be born English is to win first prize in the
lottery of life.

Cecil Rhodes

Ask any man what nationality he would prefer
to be,
and ninety-nine out of a hundred will tell you that
they would prefer to be Englishmen.

Cecil Rhodes

A French statesman, seeking to flatter Lord Palmerston,
told him, 'If I were not French, I would wish to be
English.' Palmerston replied, 'If I wasn't English, I
would wish to be English.'

Ned Sherrin, *The Oldie* magazine

England, My England

What have I done for you, England, My England?
What is there I would not do, England, my own?
With your glorious eyes austere,
As the Lord were walking near,
Whispering terrible things and dear,
As the song on your bugles blown,
England – round the world on your bugles
*   blown!*

Where shall the watchful sun, England, my England
Match the master-work you've done, England, my own?
When shall he rejoice again
Such a breed of mighty men
As come forward, one to ten,
To the song on your bugles blown,
England – down the years on your bugles blown?

Ever the faith endures, England, my England:
'Take and break us: we are yours, England, my own!
Life is good, and joy runs high
Between English earth and sky:
Death is death: but we shall die
To the song on your bugles blown
England – to the stars on your bugles blown!'

Mother of Ships whose might, England my England
Is the fierce old sea's delight, England, my own.
Chosen daughter of the Lord
Spouse-in-Chief of the ancient Sword,
There's the menace of the Word
In the song on your bugles blown,
England – out of heaven on your bugles blown!

W E Henley

Land of Lost Content

Once upon a time the English knew who they were. There was such a ready list of adjectives to hand. They were polite, unexcitable, reserved and had hot-water bottles instead of a sex life: how they reproduced was one of the mysteries of the western world. They were doers rather than thinkers, writers rather than painters, gardeners rather than cooks. They were class-bound, hidebound and incapable of expressing their emotions. They did their duty. Fortitude bordering on the incomprehensible was a byword: 'I have lost my leg, by God!' exclaimed Lord Uxbridge, as shells exploded all over the battlefield. 'By God, and have you!' replied the Duke of Wellington. A soldier lying mortally wounded in a flooded trench on the Somme was, so the myth went, likely to say only that he 'mustn't grumble'. Their most prized possession was a sense of honour. They were steadfast and trustworthy. The word of an English gentleman was as good as a bond sealed in blood.

Jeremy Paxman
The English

We must be free or die, who spake the tongue
That Shakespeare spake; the faith and morals hold
Which Milton held.

William Wordsworth

England, the Country That Dare Not Speak Its Name

Adaptability, modesty, a sense of humour and determination. These are the criteria of Britishness set out for the Great Britons Awards '04, which celebrate achievement in various areas of national life. But where did this miscellaneous set of qualities come from – and to whom do they belong?

The simple answer to that first question is that these qualities were identified by that curious modern form of camel committee, the focus group, hailing in this case from Chicago, Milan, India and bizarrely, King's Lynn. Needless to say, the group with the least clear idea of what it means to be British was the one from King's Lynn. Indeed, it was the group that seemed to think Britishness was least important, except in our country's rare moments of sporting triumph.

How did this happen? The Scots wouldn't show such uncertainty about their national characteristics. Nor would the French or Americans. The answer lies in the general weakening of English identity that took place during the emergence of the United Kingdom as a great power, as the English had to learn politeness and political correctness in order to become 'British'.

H G Wells once said that it was the glory of England to have no national dress. The overall tone of English poetry is relentlessly elegiac. In the past couple of years, that most self-consciously English of writers, Roger Scruton, has first written an 'elegy' for England and secondly announced his decision to emigrate. And yet Englishness is arguably the oldest of European nationalisms: there is a strong argument for seeing late

Anglo-Saxon England as the first nation state, with a powerful sense of national solidarity based on culture and resilient institutions. By the Council of Constance in the early 15th century, Henry V was insisting that England, by virtue of its unity of language, race and territory, counted as a great power to rival France.

All this reached a peak during the reign of Henry VIII, when the idea emerged of England alone against Papist Europe, and when the status of English as a great European language was consciously peddled. Even the first full edition of Chaucer was state-sponsored, with an introduction by Sir Brian Tuke, Henry's treasurer of the chamber (and therefore a predecessor of Gordon Brown, who has recently taken to lecturing us on Britishness). At this point, we can see English history being deliberately reworked in order to sustain Henry's claim to an authentic, autarchic national story, owing nothing to Rome.

But, just as England was the first country into industrial revolution and the first out of it, it may also have been the first to disavow nationalism. In the 16th century, everyone commented on the rabid xenophobia of the English lower classes, but already the upper classes were namby-pamby and self-effacing by comparison. We need to look more closely at the unique content of English nationalism, and in particular its individualism. As the historian and anthropologist Alan Macfarlane has argued, the English sense of individual and property rights arose out of weak family structures – weak, that is, in the sense that they were not extended families such as those of the Irish, Russians or Indians. Hence the extraordinary emphasis on 'life, liberty and property' that found expression in the works of Locke and was borrowed by the American revolution.

All that was clear enough by the early 17th century. But what happened when England found itself shunted into union with Scotland? At first, the two sides disliked each other violently. But then, in the later 18th and 19th centuries, we see a very interesting process of adaptation, in which the English back off from aggressive manifestations of identity while the Scots, Welsh and Irish ride the full tide of sentimental cultural nationalism. National poets, music, costume: they had it all. The English did not, although there was a proposal for English national costume in which men would dress in the style of Van Dyke [sic] – imagine the horror of it.

During the Victorian era, secure in the knowledge that it was the dominant political entity in the union, England encouraged this harmless behaviour by the Celtic fringe. It chose to define its nationalism in a different way, not so much by flag-waving as by playing up the idea of England as the world's greatest manufacturer, with the first parliament, the best legal system and so on. There was the British Empire, of course, but it's surprising how rarely the term 'British' was used. Well into the 20th century, prime minister Stanley Baldwin unselfconsciously used 'Englishmen' as a synonym for Britons.

It is only after the debacle of the postwar years – the loss of empire, great power status and the collapse of industry – that we see a desperate clinging on to Britishness, and attempts to stretch the concept so that, quite rightly, it could incorporate immigrants. Our confidence in being the best has simply collapsed, and that collapse is underlined by the sustained political attack directed at the traditional institutions of Crown, Church, Parliament and the law. Even the English sporting metaphor of fair play has slithered into an ill-defined and yet intolerant multiculturalism.

Hence the present confusion and weakening of English/British identity, in which certainties have been replaced by a free market in which anybody can espouse any value or none – and what better symbol of this emptiness could there be than New Labour?

Scotland, on the other hand, and to a lesser extent Wales, having kept their cultural nationalism going, have reclaimed powerful elements of their political identity and have started to develop absolutely standard European nationalisms, like those of France or Spain. All of which leaves England looking very odd: the country that dare not speak its name. And so we are thrown back on an apologetic search for the qualities that define Britishness (or do we mean Englishness?): adaptability, modesty, a sense of humour and determination. As the publicity material for Great Britons '04 so revealingly puts it, '*almost* the bulldog spirit'.

Dr David Starkey
The *Daily Telegraph*

People will not look forward to posterity, who never look backward to their ancestors.

Edmund Burke

A Patriot's Prayer

This precious island country, this verdant land sublime:
Its strengths, its laws, its charity, have stood the test of time.
No foreign land could break you or bend you to its will,
Nor puppet, slave, could make of you, or alien ways instil.
England! Oh My England! Again you stand alone,
To save your soul, your freedom, your honour and your
  throne.
Awake! You folk of England! This war will shed no blood,
But envy, greed, vindictiveness will drown you in its flood.
Arise then, dear youth of England – your hands yet hold its
  fate
And change the way the tide now flows before it is too late!

Irene Denyer, courtesy of *This England* magazine

The Georges

George the First was always reckoned
Vile, but viler George the Second;
And what mortal ever heard
Any good of George the Third?
When on earth the Fourth descended
(God be praised), the Georges ended

Walter Savage Landor

London, 1802

Wordsworth wrote this sonnet on his return from France in 1802. In disgust with the viciousness and small-mindedness he found in England, he called on Milton, one of the poets he most admired, as an example of godliness, virtue and simplicity.

Milton! thou should'st be living at this hour:
England hath need of thee: she is a fen
Of stagnant waters: altar, sword and pen,
Fireside, the heroic wealth of hall and bower,
Have forfeited their ancient English dower
Of inward happiness. We are selfish men;
Oh! raise us up, return to us again:
And give us manners, virtue, freedom, power.
Thy soul was like a Star and dwelt apart:
Thou hadst a voice whose sound was like the sea;
Pure as the naked heavens, majestic, free,
So didst thou travel on life's common way,
In cheerful godliness; and yet thy heart
The lowliest duties on itself did lay.

William Wordsworth

Our English Heritage

When I stand up for England
A thousand years are mine.
I'm one with all her heroes
Of her unbroken line.

I'm Freedom, breaking tyrants,
I'm Justice, binding wrong,
I'm Raleigh's sail borne westward,
I'm Shakespeare's golden song.

When I stand up for England,
Oh, Privilege Divine,
I'm all that man has conquered,
His thousand years are mine.

When I stand up for Goodness,
All time is in my soul,
I'm God's great Purpose starting
From Chaos to its goal.

I'm Light that moves from Darkness,
I'm Love that turns from Strife,
I'm Galilee, I'm Athens,
I'm Everlasting Life.

When I stand up for Goodness,
Oh' Privilege Divine,
I'm all that man has conquered,
His million years are mine.

Harold Begbie

The Dying Patriot

Day breaks on England down the Kentish hills,
Singing in the silence of the meadow-footing rills,
Day of my dreams, O day!
I saw them march from Dover, long ago,
With a silver cross before them, singing low,
Monks of Rome from their home where the blue seas break in
*   foam,*
Augustine with his feet of snow.

Noon strikes on England, noon on Oxford town,
– Beauty she was statue cold – there's blood upon her gown:
Noon of my dreams, O noon!
Proud and godly kings had built her, long ago,
With her towers and tombs and statues all arow,
With her fair and floral air and the love that lingers there,
And the streets where the great men go.

Sleep not, my country: tough night is here, afar
Your children of the morning are clamorous for war:
Fire in the night, O dreams!
Though she send you as she sent you, long ago,
South to desert, East to ocean, North to snow.
West of these out to seas colder than the Hebrides I must go
Where the fleet of stars is anchored and the young Star-
*   captains glow.*

James Elroy Flecker

'Slaves cannot breathe in England,' wrote William Cowper in 'The Timepiece', 'If their lungs receive our air, that moment they are free. They touch our country, and their shackles fall.'

He went on to write:

England, with all thy faults, I love thee still,
My country! And while yet a nook is left
Where English minds and manners may be found
Shall be constrained to love thee. Tho' thy clime
Be fickle, and thy year, most parts, deformed
With dripping rains, or withered by a frost,
I would not yet exchange thy sullen skies
And fields without a flower, for warmer France
With all her vines.

Be England what she will,
With all her faults, she is my country still.

Charles Churchill

Buckingham Palace

They're changing guard at Buckingham Palace –
Christopher Robin went down with Alice.
Alice is marrying one of the guard.
'A soldier's life is terrible hard,'

Says Alice.

They're changing guard at Buckingham Palace –
Christopher Robin went down with Alice.
We saw a guard in a sentry-box.
'One of the sergeants looks after their socks,'
Says Alice.

They're changing guard at Buckingham Palace –
Christopher Robin went down with Alice.
We looked for the King, but he never came.
'Well, God take care of him, all the same,'

Says Alice.

They're changing guard at Buckingham Palace –
Christopher Robin went down with Alice.
They've great big parties inside the grounds.
'I wouldn't be King for a hundred pounds,'

Says Alice.

They're changing guard at Buckingham Palace –
Christopher Robin went down with Alice.
A face looked out, but it wasn't the King's.
'He's much too busy a-signing things,'

Says Alice.

They're changing guard at Buckingham Palace –
Christopher Robin went down with Alice.
'Do you think the King knows all about me?'
'Sure to, dear, but it's time for tea,'

Says Alice.

A A Milne

The Secret People

SMILE at us, pay us, pass us; but do not quite forget;
For we are the people of England, that never have
    spoken yet.
There is many a fat farmer that drinks less cheer-
    fully,
There is many a free French peasant who is richer
    and sadder than we.
There are no folk in the whole world so helpless or
    so wise.
There is hunger in our bellies, there is laughter in
    our eyes;
You laugh at us and love us, both mugs and eyes
    are wet:
Only you do not know us. For we have not spoken
    yet.

We hear men speaking for us of new laws strong
    and sweet,
Yet is there no man speaketh as we speak in the
    street.
It may be we shall rise the last as Frenchmen rose
    the first,
Our wrath come after Russia's wrath and our wrath
    be the worst.
It may be we are meant to mark with our riot and
    our rest
God's scorn for all men governing. It may be beer
    is best.
But we are the people of England; and we have
    not spoken yet.
Smile at us, pay us, pass us. But do not quite
    forget.

G K Chesterton

The Homes of England

The stately homes of England,
*   How beautiful they stand,*
Amidst their tall ancestral trees,
*   O'er all the pleasant land!*
The deer across their greensward bound,
*   Through shade and sunny gleam;*
And the swan glides past them with the sound
*   Of some rejoicing stream.*

The merry homes of England!
*   Around their hearths by nights,*
What gladsome looks of household love
*   Meet in the ruddy light!*
There woman's voice flows forth in song,
*   Or childhood's tale is told,*
Or lips move tunefully along
*   Some glorious page of old.*

The blessed homes of England!
*   How softly on their bowers*
Is laid the holy quietness
*   That breathes from Sabbath hours!*
Solemn, yet sweet, the church-bell's chime
*   Floats through their woods at morn;*
All other sounds, in that still time,
*   Of breeze and leaf are born.*

The cottage homes of England!
  By thousands on her plains,
They are smiling o'er the silvery brooks,
  And round the hamlet fanes.
Through glowing orchards forth they peep,
  Each from its nook of leaves;
And fearless there the lowly sleep,
  As the bird beneath their eaves.

The free fair homes of England!
  Long, long in hut and hall,
May hearts of native proof be reared
  To guard each hallowed wall!
And green for ever be the groves,
  And right the flowery sod,
Where first the child's glad spirit loves
  Its country and its God!

Felicia Dorothea Hemans

Say Not the Struggle Naught Availeth

Say not the struggle naught availeth,
    The labour and the wounds are vain,
The enemy faints not, nor faileth,
    And as things have been, things remain.

If hopes were dupes, fears may be liars;
    It may be, in yon smoke concealed,
Your comrades chase e'en now the fliers,
    And, but for you, possess the field.

For while the tired waves, vainly breaking,
    Seem here no painful inch to gain,
Far back through creeks and inlets making
    Comes silent, flooding in, the main.

And not by eastern windows only,
    When daylight comes, comes in the light;
In front the sun climbs slow, how slowly,
    But westward, look, the land is bright!

Arthur Hugh Clough

Vitaï Lampada

There's a breathless hush in the Close to-night –
Ten to make and the match to win –
A bumping pitch and a blinding light,
An hour to play and the last man in.
And it's not for the sake of a ribboned coat,
Or the selfish hope of a season's fame,
But his Captain's hand on his shoulder smote –
'Play up! play up! And play the game!'

The sand of the desert is sodden red, –
Red with the wreck of a square that broke; –
The Gatling's jammed and the Colonel dead,
And the regiment blind with dust and smoke.
The river of death has brimmed his banks,
And England's far, and Honour a name,
But the voice of a schoolboy rallies the ranks:
'Play up! play up! and play the game!'

This is the word that year by year,
While in her place the School is set,
Every one of her sons must hear,
And none that hears it dare forget.
This they all with a joyful mind
Bear through life like a torch in flame,
And falling fling to the host behind –
'Play up! play up! and play the game!'

Henry Newbolt

The Rolling English Road

Before the Roman came to Rye or out to Severn strode,
The rolling English drunkard made the rolling English road.
A reeling road, a rolling road, that rambles round the shire,
And after him the parson ran, the sexton and the squire;
A merry road, a mazy road, and such as we did tread
The night we went to Birmingham by way of Beachy Head.

I knew no harm of Bonaparte and plenty of the Squire,
And for to fight the Frenchman I did not much desire;
But I did bash their baggonets because they came array'd
To straighten out the crooked road an English drunkard
*   made,*
Where you and I went down the lane with ale-mugs in our
*   hands,*
The night we went to Glastonbury by way of Goodwin
*   Sands.*

His sins they were forgiven him; or why do flowers run
Behind him; and the hedges all strengthening in the sun?
The wild thing went from left to right and knew not which
*   was which,*
But the wild rose was above him when they found him in
*   the ditch.*
God pardon us, nor harden us; we did not see so clear
The night we went to Bannockburn by way of Brighton Pier.

My friends, we will not go again or ape an ancient rage,
Or stretch the folly of our youth to be the shame of age,
But walk with clearer eyes and ears this path that wandereth,
And see undrugg'd in evening light the decent inn of death;
For there is good news yet to hear and fine things to be
   seen,
Before we go to Paradise by way of Kensal Green.

G K Chesterton

Upon Westminster Bridge

Earth has not anything to show more fair:
Dull would he be of soul who could pass by
A sight so touching in its majesty:
This City now doth, like a garment, wear
The beauty of the morning; silent, bare,
Ships, towers, domes, theatres, and temples lie
Open unto the fields, and to the sky;
All bright and glittering in the smokeless air.
Never did sun more beautifully steep
In his first splendour, valley, rock, or hill;
Ne'er saw I, never felt, a calm so deep!
The river glideth at his own sweet will:
Dear God! the very houses seem asleep;
And all that mighty heart is lying still!

William Wordsworth

Mrs Beeton wrote a book
Teaching women how to cook
Judging by what I've just eaten
Mother's cooking can't be beeton.

Anon

English Cooking

The history of England is its cooking. Successive invaders to English shores, Roman, Viking and Norman, naturally introduced their own culinary traditions to the native cuisine. The returning Crusaders introduced Arab influences too, adding dried fruits and aromatic spices to both sweet and savoury dishes. Other costly, new and luxurious foodstuffs such as sugar, almonds and citrus fruits were also imported from exotic lands in vast quantities in the Middle Ages. Such foods became the newly fashionable status symbols of a rich and self-indulgent elite and were used lavishly in the great feasts of the time.

The reputation of our once great national cuisine, which in the past was universally admired for the sheer diversity of its ingredients and imaginative cooking, deserves to be revived and restored to its former glory. Our traditional recipes should be national treasures. They have come down to us from the kitchens of the great aristocratic houses, humble cottages and city streets, where they were lovingly and skilfully created. We should cherish them as we would a piece of fine china or antique furniture. Such recipes are a valuable part of our heritage which is slowly and surely being forgotten . . . and if that is allowed to happen, it would be a tragedy.

Richard, Earl of Bradford. *Porters English Cookery Bible*

The Roast Beef of Old England

When mighty roast Beef was the Englishman's *Food,*
It ennobled our Hearts, and enriched our Blood;
Our Soldiers were brave, and our Courtiers were good.
   Oh the Roast Beef of Old England,
   And Old England's *Roast Beef!*

Then, Britons, *from all nice Dainties refrain,*
Which effeminate Italy, France *and* Spain;
And mighty Roast Beef shall command on the Main.
   Oh the Roast Beef, &c.

Henry Fielding

'O the Roast Beef of Old England' (1748, Tate Gallery) is the title by which Hogarth's painting *The Gate of Calais* is commonly known. Painted after Hogarth had been arrested in Calais, suspected of being an English spy, it is a profoundly jingoistic statement by the outraged artist, who is seen sketching in the background. The central incident is the arrival of a succulent side of English beef, the sight of which is causing a fat Catholic friar and starving French soldiers to slaver with desire and admiration.

From A Christmas Carol

 There never was such a goose. Bob said he didn't believe there ever was such a goose cooked. Its tenderness and flavour, size and cheapness, were the themes of universal admiration. Eked out by apple-sauce and mashed pota-
toes, it was a sufficient dinner for the whole family; indeed, as Mrs Cratchit said with great delight (surveying one small atom of a bone upon the dish), they hadn't ate it all at last! Yet every one had had enough, and the youngest Cratchits in particular, were steeped in sage and onion to the eyebrows! But now, the plates being changed by Miss Belinda, Mrs Cratchit left the room alone – too nervous to bear witnesses – to take the pudding up and bring it in.

Suppose it should not be done enough! Suppose it should break in turning out! Suppose somebody should have got over the wall of the back-yard, and stolen it, while they were merry with the goose – a supposition at which the two young Cratchits became livid! All sorts of horrors were supposed.

Hallo! A great deal of steam! The pudding was out of the copper. A smell like a washing-day! That was the cloth. A smell like an eating-house and a pastrycook's next door to each other, with a laundress's next door to that! That was the pudding! In half a minute Mrs Cratchit entered – flushed, but smiling proudly – with the pudding, like a speckled cannon-ball, so hard and firm, blazing in half of half-a-quartern of ignited brandy, and bedight with Christmas holly stuck into the top.

Oh, a wonderful pudding! Bob Cratchit said, and calmly too, that he regarded it as the greatest success achieved by Mrs Cratchit since their marriage. Mrs Cratchit said that now the weight was off her mind, she would confess she had had her doubts about the quantity of flour. Everybody had something to say about it, but nobody said or thought it was at all a small pudding for a large family. It would have been flat heresy to do so. Any Cratchit would have blushed to hint at such a thing.

Charles Dickens

Sir Loin

The word sirloin comes from the French word '*surloynge*' – '*sur*', meaning over, and '*loynge*', meaning loin. It refers to the upper part of the hind loin, which makes a fine roast joint.

There is a nice story that the word sirloin came about from a knighting by an English king, and Thomas Fuller, writing in 1655, ascribes it to Henry VIII. However, it is more likely that the king in question was James I. The incident is recorded as having taken place at Hoghton Tower in Lancashire. In 1611 the de Hoghtons were made the premier baronets in the country and were entertaining James I to lunch. Coming into the banqueting hall, the King saw a superb loin of beef. Tradition has it that he drew his short sword and told the Hoghton pages to bring the beef to him. They went down on their knees and the King said, 'Arise, Sir Loin'.

The present head of the family and 14th baronet, Sir Bernard de Hoghton, says that sources for this account include the King's diarist, Nicholas Ashton, and a sketch by a court painter.

To a Goose

If thou didst feed on western plains of yore;
Or waddle wide with flat and flabby feet
Over some Cambrian mountain's plashy moor;
Or find in farmer's yard a safe retreat
From gypsy thieves, and foxes sly and fleet;
If thy grey quills, by lawyer guided, trace
Deeds big with ruin to some wretched race,
Or love-sick poet's sonnet, sad and sweet,
Wailing the rigour of his lady fair;
Or if, the drudge of housemaid's daily toil,
Cobwebs and dust thy pinions white besoil,
Departed Goose! I neither know nor care.
But this I know, that we pronounced thee fine,
Seasoned with sage and onions, and port wine.

Robert Southey

Woe to the cook whose sauce has no sting.

Geoffrey Chaucer

Recipe for a Salad

To make this condiment, your poet begs
The pounded yellow of two hard-boiled eggs;
Two boiled potatoes, passed through kitchen-sieve,
Smoothness and softness to the salad give;
Let onion atoms lurk within the bowl,
And, half-suspected, animate the whole.
Of mordant mustard add a single spoon,
Distrust the condiment that bites so soon;
But deem it not, thou man of herbs, a fault,
To add a double quantity of salt.
And, lastly, o'er the flavoured compound toss
A magic soup-spoon of anchovy sauce.
Oh, green and glorious! Oh, herbaceous treat!
'T would tempt the dying anchorite to eat;
Back to the world he'd turn his fleeting soul,
And plunge his fingers in the salad bowl!
Serenely full, the epicure would say,
Fate can not harm me, I have dined to-day!

Sidney Smith

The golden rule of reading a menu – if you can't pronounce it, you can't afford it.

Frank Muir

Adlestrop

Yes, I remember Adlestrop –
The name, because one afternoon
Of heat the express-train drew up there
Unwontedly. It was late June.

The steam hissed. Someone cleared his
    throat.
No one left and no one came
On the bare platform. What I saw
Was Adlestrop – only the name

And willows, willow-herb, and grass,
And meadowsweet, and haycocks dry,
No whit less still and lonely fair
Than the high cloudlets in the sky.

And for that minute a blackbird sang
Close by, and round him, mistier,
Farther and farther, all the birds
Of Oxfordshire and Gloucestershire.

Edward Thomas

Not Adlestrop

Not Adlestrop, no – besides, the name
hardly matters. Nor did I languish in June heat.
Simply, I stood, too early, on the empty platform,
and the wrong train came in slowly, surprised, stopped.
Directly facing me, from a window,
a very, very pretty girl leaned out.

When I, all instinct,
stared at her, she, all instinct, inclined her head away
as if she'd divined the much married life in me,
or as if she might spot, up platform,
some unlikely familiar.

For my part, under the clock, I continued
my scrutiny with unmitigated pleasure.
And she knew it, she certainly knew it, and would not
glance at me in the silence of not Adlestrop.

Only when the train heaved noisily, only
when it jolted, when it slid away, only then,
daring and secure, she smiled back at my smile,
and I, daring and secure, waved back at her waving.
And so it was, all the way down the hurrying platform
as the train gathered atrocious speed
towards Oxfordshire or Gloucestershire.

Dannie Abse

From **Prothalamion**

At length they all to merry London came,
    To merry London, my most kindly nurse,
    That to me gave this life's first native source,
Though from another place I take my name,
    An house of ancient fame:
There when they came whereas those bricky towers
    The which on Thames' broad aged back do ride,
Where now the studious lawyers have their bowers,
    There whilome wont the Templar-knights to bide,
        Till they decay'd through pride;
Next whereunto there stands a stately place,
Where oft I gained gifts and goodly grace
    Of that great lord, which therein wont to dwell,
Whose want to well now feels my friendless case;
    But ah! here fits not well
    Old woes, but joys, to tell
Against the bridal day, which is not long:
Sweet Thames! Run softly, till I end my song.

Edmund Spenser

Forget six counties overhung with smoke,
Forget the snorting steam and piston stroke,
Forget the spreading of the hideous town;
Think rather of the packhorse on the down,
And dream of London, small and white and clean,
The clear Thames bordered by its gardens green.

William Morris

From My Oxford – John Mortimer

After London ('merry London, my most kindly nurse', as Spenser called it), nowhere typifies England better than Oxford, the City of Dreaming Spires. In this extract from *My Oxford*, a student view of Oxford in wartime, John Mortimer paints a fascinating picture of under-graduate life at that great university during the Second World War.

The high life of Oxford, of course, was something I had never encountered when I moved into my rooms in Meadow Buildings. To my dismay I found I was sharing them with Parsons, a tall man with bicycle clips and a pronounced Adam's apple who tried to lure me into the Bible Society. One night my friend Oliver and I tried the effect of boiling up Algerian wine, college sherry and a bottle of Bols he had stolen from his mother's dressing-case, in Parson's electric kettle. Oliver's mother was an ageless South American who moved in an aura of patchouli and poodles round a series of rented flats with white wrought-iron furniture in the area of Charles Street. Perhaps for this reason Oliver saw himself as an eighteenth-century English squire and this extraordinary brew was meant to be punch, or hot toddy, or whatever eighteenth-century squires drank in the evenings. When I recovered from the draught I found Parsons wearing cycle clips and kneeling over me in prayer: I also heard from down the corridor Brahms's Fourth Symphony like music from some remote paradise.

In fact, my memory of Oxford seems, looking back over a vast distance, to consist almost entirely of Brahms's Fourth Symphony, a piece of music of which I have become decreasingly fond, as I have lost the taste for bow ties, Balkan Sobranie cigarettes, and sherry and Bols boiled up in an electric kettle. But that music came from the room of someone who really did affect my life and of whom I still think with gratitude and bewilderment, remembering his serene life and extraordinary death.

My father, to whom I owe so much, never told me the difference between right and wrong; now I think that's why I remain so greatly in his debt. But Henry Winter, who slowly and with enormous care sharpened a thorn needle with sandpaper to play Brahms on his huge horned gramophone, became a kind of yardstick, not of taste but of moral behaviour. He had no doubt whatever about the war: he was against it. He looked forward to the call-up, the refusal, the arguments with the tribunals and the final consignment to Pentonville or the Fire Service with amused calm. He read classics, I mean actually *read* them. He would sit in a squeaking basket chair, smoking a pipe and giving me his version of chunks of Homer and Euripides which up to then I had been trained to regard as almost insoluble crossword puzzles or grammarians' equations with no recognizable human content. I was born of tone deaf parents and, in the school songs, I was instructed to open and shut my mouth soundlessly so that no emergent discord might mar the occasion. Yet Winter slowly, painstakingly, introduced me to music, and the pleasure I now take in it is due entirely to him.

Winter's rejection of violence, and what seemed to me the extraordinary gentle firmness of his moral stance, was no result of religious conviction. He was courageously sceptical, fearlessly agnostic, open and reasonable, with none of the tormented Christianity of my ex-room mate. Parsons had applied for a transfer after the desecration of his electric kettle and left me in solitary possession of a huge Gothic sitting-room and a bedroom the size of a waiting-room at St Pancras, with a chipped wash basin in which I kept a smoked salmon caught by my aunt in Devon and in defiance of rationing.

I suppose Oxford's greatest gift is friendship, for which there is all the time in the world. After Oxford there are love affairs, marriages, working relationships, manipulations, lifelong enemies: but even then, in rationed, blacked-out Oxford, there were limitless hours for talking, drinking, staying up all night, even going for walks (how many years is it since I went for a walk?) with a friend. Winter and I were emerging from the chrysalis of schoolboy homosexuality; and the girls we preferred were notably boyish. Veronica Lake rather than Betty Grable, and Katherine Hepburn in *Philadelphia Story* who, Frank Hauser told us, was the natural bridge into the heterosexual world. At first the girls we loved were tennis-playing virgins, posed, like Proust's androgynous heroines, forever unobtainable against a background of parks and carrying string bags full of Slazengers. There is nothing like sexual frustration to give warmth to friendship, which is why it flourishes in prisons, armies, on Arctic expeditions and did well in wartime in Oxford. Winter and I became inseparable, and when, as time went on, I began to do things without him, I felt, for a moment quite strongly, guilty twinges of infidelity.

And now, from one of the best-loved living English authors to one of its best-loved humorists – Alan Coren has a very different take on Oxford.

A Credit to Oxford

When, not so very long ago, the credit card slipped into our lives and changed them for ever, it was able to do so by making us one simple promise. It had pondered long and hard about that promise, because it had to be a very good promise indeed if we were to be persuaded that changing our lives for ever was the right thing to do, and the credit card knew that this end could not be achieved by promising us that we should always have something to scrape the ice off our windscreens, or free our molar gaps from raspberry pips, or clear crumbs from our tablecloths or even break into premises by opening locks to which we lacked the key. It knew that it had to reach far deeper into the collective psyche to locate and fondle that sub-conscious G-spot which would make it irresistible to us.

So the credit card promised that it would say more about us than cash ever could. For it had concluded that what we most wanted the world to say about us was that we had so much money that we didn't need money at all, because an organisation with more money than anybody had such trust in us that it would pick up any tab on our behalf. All we had to do when the tab was presented was lay the card beside it whereupon our creditor would immediately fall to the Axminster and kiss our hems.

After a bit, of course, once that wondrous status had been conferred on so many punters that its wondrous-ness was inevitably diminished, new wondrousness had to be introduced, first by the gold card then by the platinum, each saying even more about us than cash ever could. It now said that we were not just rich, but so rich that we had to be someone a bit special to have got that rich in the first place.

At which point the credit card suddenly discovered it had run out of precious metals. This was a serious problem: with more and more platinum cards about, more and more rich people wanted even more said about them than mere platinum ever could, but there were no superior ones available to say it. What was the credit card to do?

I'll tell you what it was to do. It was to send me a brochure. It hit my mat this morning. On the cover is a picture of The University of Oxford Visa card. Open the brochure, and inside you will find two dozen pictures of college Visa cards, alongside a smarmy rubric declaring that you can now apply for a Magdalen Visa card, a Balliol card, a Wadham card, and so on. I rang Visa. No, I didn't need to have been at any of these colleges to qualify, all I needed to have was the cash which the card would say more about me than. And since a tiny percentage of each transaction goes to the college, what it patently says is that the bearer is supporting his *alma mater*. He is an Oxford man. Watch waiters fawn! Watch osteopaths goggle! Watch checkout lovelies swoon!

I shall not, of course, be applying for any of these, since for some irritating reason All Souls has not signed up to the scheme, and theirs is the only card I'd want to flash apart from the Rowing Blue Visa card, which, sadly, isn't offered, either. I shall just have to bide my time, until the next inevitable status-hike. It might well bring the Eton Visa card and I shouldn't mind one of those. It would knock their socks off at Cricklewood Donuts. Either that or the Brigade of Guards Visa card, ticketyboo for buying a James Locke bowler, they'd probably chuck in a bespoke baseball cap gratis and bow you to the tinkling door, very nice.

Not, mind, that there isn't one tiny snag to all this, already spotted, I'm sure, by anyone unsettled at the prospect of being spotted; for while it is one thing to plonk down your impressive plastic in Crockfords or Asprey's or some equally public arena, it is quite another to have it clocked by someone who immediately bellows: 'Good God, a Wykehamist, which house, which year, did you have old Ratty ffolkes-Simcox for Greek, too?' or 'Stone me, a 2 para Visa card, we must have been at Goose Green together, come and have a large one!'

For that, I'm afraid, is the inbuilt curse of the credit card's latest quantum leap. It now says more about you than truth ever can.

Alan Coren
The Cricklewood Tapestry

Sea Fever

I must down to the sea again, to the lonely sea and the sky,
And all I ask is a tall ship and a star to steer her by,
And the wheel's kick and the wind's song and the white
    sail's shaking,
And a grey mist on the sea's face and the grey dawn breaking.

I must down to the sea again, for the call of the running tide
Is a wild call and a clear call that may not be denied;
And all I ask is a windy day with the white clouds flying,
And the flung spray and the blown spume, and the seagulls
    crying.

I must down to the sea again, to the vagrant gypsy life.
To the gull's way and the whale's way where the wind's like
      a whetted knife:
And all I ask is a merry yarn from a laughing fellow-rover
And quiet sleep and a sweet dream when the long trick's over.

John Masefield

From The Deserted Village

A time there was, ere England's griefs began,
When every rood of ground maintained its man;
For him light labour spread her wholesome store,
Just gave what life required, but gave no more.
His best companions, innocence and health;
And his best riches, ignorance of wealth.

But times are altered; trade's unfeeling train
Usurp the land and dispossess the swain;
Along the lawn, where scattered hamlets rose,
Unwieldy wealth, and cumbrous pomp repose;
And every want to opulence allied,
And every pang that folly pays to pride.
These gentle hours that plenty bade to bloom,
Those calm desires that asked but little room,
Those healthful sports that graced the peaceful scene,
Lived in each look, and brightened all the green;
These far departing seek a kinder shore,
And rural mirth and manners are no more.

Oliver Goldsmith

With Dignity and Calm

With dignity and calm, but debonair,
He left the awed pavilion, head in air,
His gear and garments faultlessly assembled.
His shirt was silken, pen could never trace
The beauty of his trousers' matchless grace
And as he walked to his appointed place,
The bowlers trembled.

The wicket reached, he eyed the umpires hard,
With most elaborate caution took his guard,
Made a hole, then ground his heel within it.
While the field grew tremulous and pale
He banged it, he poked it, he measured it to scale,
And then he went and scratched it with a bail
For quite a minute.

This done, the pitch he viewed with care,
A speck of dust removing here and there;
Prodding and sweeping, hammering and patting,
The wicket-keeper looking on aghast.
He made the buckles of his leg-guards fast,
Adjusted his gloves, and seemed disposed at last
To think of batting.

Not yet. Unblushingly he now began
To note the fielders, studying every man
With keen regard, as if each only mattered.
But in the end he took his stance, his brow
Showed keen resolve. He faced the bowler, now.
There came a horrid row–
His stumps were scattered.

4 8

With dignity he made his way
Back to the dumb pavilion.
I must say his mien was proud, his gait was firm and steady,
And as upon the scoring-board they stuck,
With callous haste, a large and hideous duck,
He said, in high clear accent, 'What putrid luck,
I wasn't ready'.

Anon

Stumps Drawn

He played his cricket on the heath,
The pitch was full of bumps;
A fast ball hit him in the teeth,
The dentist drew the stumps.

Anon

St George,
He Was For England

Today, I saw St George's Flag
fluttering from a mast,
It waved in recognition
to the glories of the past.
It beckoned to the future,
and seemed to say aloud,
'If you should be An Englishman
Look Up . . . my Son . . . be proud',
Let Hope still be your anvil
and Courage be your forge . . .
and, come what may
let Men still say . . .
      GOD FOR ELIZABETH . . .
          . . . ENGLAND . . .
             AND, ST GEORGE.

Charlie Chester MBE

St George and The Dragon

The legends surrounding St George are very varied. One of them concerns the famous dragon, with which he is invariably portrayed. According to legend, a pagan town in Libya was being terrorised by a dragon. To placate it, the locals kept throwing it sheep, and when it still remained unsatisfied, they began sacrificing some of the citizenry. Finally, the local princess was to be thrown to the beast also, but Good St George came along, slaughtered the dragon and rescued the fair princess. At this the townsfolk converted to Christianity.

Legends apart, the true story of St George begins when George was born of Christian parents at Lydda in the Vale of Sharon (Palestine), about AD270. He served as an officer in the Roman Army under the Emperor, Diocletian. When Diocletian's successor, Caesar Galerius (often described as 'the wickedest man in the world') issued edicts against Christians, George tore them up and refused to throw incense on a lamp before the Emperor's statue, declaring, 'I believe in Jesus Christ, who only is both God and Lord.' St Ambrose of Milan, whose account of St George's martyrdom is one of the most trustworthy, tells us:

'George, the most faithful soldier of Jesus Christ, when religion was by others concealed, alone adventured to confess the Name of God, whose heavenly grace infused such constancy into him that he not only warned the tyrants, but was contemptuous of their torture.'

For his obduracy, George was condemned to death and beheaded on 23 April 303 and this date has ever since been kept as his feast day in Heaven.

During the Crusades, at the Siege of Jerusalem, Richard I, the Lion Heart, claimed to have seen a vision of St George bearing a red-cross banner. Although he himself did not enter Jerusalem with the victorious army (declaring himself unworthy to do so), in gratitude for the victory he repaired the church over the grave of St George at Lydda, and there took the saint as his personal patron. In 1220 Henry III ordered the Feast of St George, 23 April, to be placed in the calendar of nationally observed special days.

Edward III founded the Order of the Garter in 1348 under the patronage of St George. In 1399 Archibishop Arundel called a Synod at St Paul's to receive a petition from the clergy that read:

'The feast of St George the Martyr, who is the spiritual patron of England, should be appointed to be solemnised throughout England and observed as a holiday, even as other nations observe the feast of their patron.'

It was at the Siege of Harfleur that Henry V rallied his troops with the great battlecry immortalised by Shakespeare: 'God for Harry, England and St George!'

The Royal Society of St George

It gives me great pleasure to have been invited to contribute to this book in my position as the Chairman of The Royal Society of St George. The Royal Society of St George has existed in England since 1894, although various organisations of St George have been present in this country since the Middle Ages. The Society was granted a Royal Charter by Her Majesty Queen Elizabeth II in 1983 and the instructions of that Charter require that the Society should:

i Foster the love of England and strengthen England and the Commonwealth by spreading the knowledge of English history, traditions and ideals.

ii Keep fresh the memory of those in all walks of life who have served England or the Commonwealth in the past, in order to inspire leadership in the future.

iii Combat all activities likely to undermine the strength of England or the Commonwealth.

iv Further English interests everywhere to ensure that St George's Day is properly celebrated and to provide focal points all the world over where English men and women may gather together.

The Society now has one hundred branches worldwide, fifty in England and fifty overseas, and is increasing in membership as Englishmen of all religions once again begin to value the uniqueness of their long history and worldwide influence. It is easy to appreciate, therefore, our enthusiasm for this book, for it not only honours the writers and orators who are included, but reminds us all of our remarkable past. I hope you enjoy reading it.

John C Clemence QPM
Chairman
The Royal Society of St George

St George – Knight of Lydda

Shines here the shrine of noble martyr, George,
Whose fame is spread throughout the whole wide world.
Proclaiming Christ as Lord, in spite of bonds,
And prison, hunger, thirst and searing flame,
He raised his head to dwell amidst the stars.

Entombed, in honour, 'neath the eastern skies,
Lo, beneath western stars his aid is sought.
Therefore, lift up your hearts and pay your vows,
For here, true faith will win the boon it craves.
Let then the souls that Christ's new temples are
Advance along the same straight way as George.

Venantius Fortunatus (530–610), Bishop of Poitiers
De Basilica Sancti Georgii

Anthem to St George

Verse   Here's to Saint George's Name,
         It burns a flame,
         To glorify old England's name,
         And here's to the pride of those
         Who wear the English Rose.

Chorus England, my England
         My green and pleasant homeland,
         There is no other land
         Can mean as much to me . . .
         None shall divide us,
         And with St George to guide us
         Cry . . . God Bless Elizabeth . . .
         And . . . ENGLAND.

Verse   Land of the mighty oak,
         And sturdy folk,
         Whose spirit never shall be broken
         Proud of our destiny
         Forever to be free.

Chorus England, my England
         My green and pleasant homeland,
         There is no other land
         Can mean as much to me . . .
         None shall divide us,
         And with St George to guide us
         Cry . . . God Bless Elizabeth . . .
         And . . . ENGLAND.

Charlie Chester M B E

The Spirit of St George

There stands the gracious parish church,
There, too, the blacksmith's forge,
There grows the solid oak and ash,
For England and Saint George

All he stands for still remains
In this England of today –
Let us merge in faith and strength
And each a dragon slay.
For there are many dragons –
Injustice, moral decay –
Because of which so many have,
Sadly, lost their way.

There rise the hills, there flows the streams
Yonder fall valley and gorge,
There roll the green and daisied fields
Of England and Saint George.

Dressed in blossom, white and pink,
Our English orchards stand,
Neath the trees sheep quietly graze
On lush green meadowland.
The sleepy village roofed in thatch
Unchanged since days of old,
Men till and sow in modernway
And reap their harvest gold.

With love of country, love of God,
Together ahead we'll forge
To safeguard our inheritance
The spirit of Saint George.

Barbara Jemison

From An Ode for St George's Day

One of Southey's laureate poems, this ode is full of patriotic sentiment, with its many references to earlier successes against the French – at Crécy and Poitiers and Agincourt, where Henry V led his men to a great victory on St George's Day, 23 April 1415.

> . . . But thou, O England! to that sainted name
> Hast given its proudest praise, its loftiest fame.
>   Witness the field of Cressy, on that day,
>   When volleying thunders roll'd unheard on high,
>   For in that memorable fray
>   Broken, confused, and scatter'd in dismay,
>   France had ears only for the Conqueror's cry,
> St. George, St. George for England! St. George
>   and Victory!

> Bear witness Poitiers! where again the foe
> From that same hand received his overthrow.
>   In vain essay'd, Mount Joye St Denis rang
>   From many a boastful tongue,
>   And many a hopeful heart in onset brave;
>   Their courage in the shock of battle quail'd
>   His dread response when sable Edward gave,
>   And England and St George again prevail'd.

Bear witness Agincourt, where once again
The bannered lilies on the ensanguin'd plain
 Were trampled by the fierce pursuers' feet;
  And France, doom'd ever to defeat
Against that foe, beheld her myriads fly
 Before the withering cry,
St George, St George for England! St George
   and Victory!

 That cry in many a field of Fame
 Through glorious ages held its high renown;
Nor less hath Britain proved the sacred name
   Auspicious to her crown.
  Troubled too oft her course of fortune ran
   Till when the Georges came
    Her happiest age began.
  Beneath their just and liberal sway,
  Old feuds and factions died away;

 One feeling through her realms were known,
 One interest of the Nation and the Throne.
Ring, then, ye bells upon St George's Day,
From every tower in glad accordance ring;
And let all instruments, full, strong, or sweet,
   With touch of modulated string,
 And soft of swelling breath, and sonorous beat,
   The happy name repeat,
While heart and voice their joyous tribute bring
 And speak the People's love for George their King.

Robert Southey

Part of the speech by Sir Stanley Baldwin to the Annual Dinner of The Royal Society of St George, 6 May 1924.

Now, I have very little more that I want to say to you to-night, but on an occasion like this, I suppose there is no one who does not ask himself in his heart and is a little shy of expressing it, what it is that England stands for to him, and to her. And there comes into my mind a wonder as to what England may stand for in the minds of generations to come if our country goes on during the next generation as she has done in the last two, in seeing her fields converted into towns.

To me, England is the country, and the country is England. And when I ask myself what I mean by England, when I think of England when I am abroad, England comes to me through my various senses – through the ear, through the eye, and through certain imperishable scents. I will tell you what they are, and there may be those among you who feel as I do.

The sounds of England: the tinkle of the hammer on the anvil in the country smithy, the corncrake on a dewy morning, the sound of the scythe against the whetstone, and the sight of a plough team coming over the brow of a hill, the sight that has been seen in England since England was a land, and may be seen in England long after the Empire has perished and every works in England has ceased to function, for centuries the one eternal sight of England. The wild anemones in the woods in April, the last load at night of hay being drawn down a lane as the twilight comes on, when you can scarcely distinguish the figures of the horses as they take it home to the farm, and above all, most subtle, most penetrating and most moving, the smell of wood smoke coming up in an autumn evening, or the smell of the scutch fires: that wood smoke that our ancestors, tens of thousands of years ago, must have caught on the air when they were coming home with the result of the day's forage, when they were still nomads, and when they were still roaming the forests and the plains of the continent of Europe. These things strike down into the very depths of our nature, and touch chords that go back to the beginning of time and the human race, but they are chords that with every year of our life sound a deeper note in our innermost being.

These are the things that make England, and I grieve for it that they are not the childish inheritance of the majority of the people to-day in our country. They ought to be the inheritance of every child born into this country, but nothing can be more touching than to see how the working man and woman after generations in the towns will have their tiny bit of garden if they can, will go to gardens if they can, to look at something they have never seen as children, but which their ancestors knew and loved. The love of these things is innate and inherent in our people. It makes for that love of home, one of the strongest features of our race, and it is that that makes our race seek its new home in the Dominions overseas, where they have room to see things like this that they can no more see at home. It is that power of making homes, almost peculiar to our people, and it is one of the sources of their greatness. They go overseas, and they take with them what they learned at home: love of justice, love of truth, and the broad humanity that are so characteristic of English people. It may well be that these traits on which we pride ourselves, which we hope to show and try to show in our own lives, may survive – survive among our people so long as they are a people – and I hope and believe this, that just as to-day more than fifteen centuries since the last of those great Roman legionaries left England, we still speak of the

Roman strength, and the Roman work, and the Roman character, so perhaps in the ten thousandth century, long after the Empires of this world as we know them have fallen and others have risen and fallen, and risen and fallen again, the men who are then on this earth may yet speak of those characteristics which we prize as the characteristics of the English, and that long after, maybe, the name of the country has passed away, wherever men are honourable and upright and persevering, lovers of home, of their brethren, of justice and of humanity, the men in the world of that day may say, 'We still have among us the gifts of that great English race.'

St George and the Order of the Garter

The Most Noble Order of the Garter is England's highest order of chivalry and was founded in 1348 by King Edward III. The Order consists of Her Majesty the Queen, who is Sovereign of the Order, HRH the Prince of Wales and 24 Knights Companion.

The origin of the symbolic Blue Garter with the words, 'Honi Soit Qui Mal Y Pense' will probably never be known for certain, as the earliest records of the Order were destroyed by fire. Popular myth has it that it started at a ball held at Calais. It is said that Joan, Countess of Salisbury, dropped her garter and, seeing her embarrassment, King Edward picked it up and bound it about his own leg, saying in French, 'Shamed be he who evil thinks'.

The more likely historical truth is that when Edward III decided to instigate an Order of Chivalry, he chose the symbol of the garter because the garter was a small strap to attach armour and it might have been thought appropriate to use it as a symbol of binding together in common brotherhood. The garter was also the leather sword-belt that held the sword with which a knight was invested, and from which we get the term, 'a belted earl'.

St George's Chapel, Windsor, is the spiritual home of the Order and the banners of the knights hang in the Quire while oak panelling bears the crests of all former members of the Order. St George's Hall at Windsor Castle, now beautifully restored to its former glory following the tragic fire of 1992, also has the arms of 700 past Knights of the Garter emblazoned on the oak panels of the vaulted ceiling.

Each June, members of the Order assemble and don the mantle of the Order and the premier badge, the 'Greater George', and walk in procession to the Chapel wearing the full robes of the Order, including dark blue velvet hat with white plumes – a splendid sight which attracts thousands of onlookers each year.

St George and the Royal Rolls-Royce

The mascot on the radiator cap of all Rolls-Royce cars has, from its inception, been the 'Spirit of Ecstasy' – all bar one, that is. The Rolls-Royce in which Her Majesty the Queen is travelling has a model of St George on a horse poised victoriously over a slain dragon. Designed by the artist Edward Seago and cast in silver, it can be transferred from car to car, as necessary, but is most often used on the Rolls-Royce Phantom VI, which was presented to the Queen on her Silver Jubilee in 1978 by the Society of Motor Manufacturers and Traders.

The Spirit of England

The Honourable Artillery Company, St George's Day Dinner, London, and Broadcast, 23 April 1953

England has a quality that no one should overlook. England, like nature, never draws a line without smudging it. We lack the sharp logic of some other countries whom in other ways we greatly admire – in our climate, the atmosphere is veiled, there are none of these sharp presentations, and although we have our differences – especially as in a few minutes I have to go back to the House of Commons – I won't say are slaves to differences, but at any rate present the point of view which we hold. We have our differences but they do not divide us as they do in nearly all the other countries of the world. There is a great underlying spirit of neighbourliness and there is without doubt a very strong common sense of our national unity and life that, though it doesn't help us in the small matters with which we have to deal from day to day, may well be our salvation in our troubles.

Nothing can save England, if she will not save herself. If we lose faith in ourselves, in our capacity to guide and govern, if we lose our will to live, then, indeed, our story is told. If, while on all sides foreign nations are every day asserting a more aggressive and militant nationalism by arms and trade – if we remain paralysed by our own theoretical doctrines or plunged in the stupor of after-war exhaustion – but this is twenty years ago, this is not new – indeed, all that the croakers predict will come true and our ruin will be certain and final.

But why should we break up the solid structure of British power founded upon so much help, kindliness, and freedom? Why should we break it up for dreams which may some day come true, but now are only dreams, or it may be nightmares? We ought as a nation and Empire – you won't mind my mentioning that word? – I didn't get shouted down when I said it twenty years ago tonight – Empire, we might, we ought, to weather any storm that blows at least as well as any other existing system of human government.

We are at once more experienced and more truly united than any people in the world. It may well be, I say, that the most glorious chapters in our history are yet to be written. Indeed, the very problems and dangers that encompass us in our country ought to make English men and women of this generation glad to be here at such a time. We ought to rejoice at the responsibilities with which destiny has honoured us and be proud that we are the guardians of our country in an age when her life is at stake. I have lived, since then, to see our country accomplish, achieve her finest hour and I have no doubt that if this spirit of England continues, there is no reason at all why twenty years hence someone may not stand at the table of this ancient company and speak in the sense of pride and hope in which I have ventured to address you tonight.

Sir Winston Churchill

A century ago, a little girl, who was to become Mrs
Clifford Mills, author of the patriotic children's story
and play, *Where the Rainbow Ends*, noted that St George's
Day was not celebrated as it should be. She wrote:

Alas for St George of England
The valiant knight of old,
Who slew the fiery dragon
And of whom many tales are told.
Although he is our Patron Saint
We think nought of his day,
And there is silence everywhere
Where there ought to be grand display.

In April 2004 the Spy column of the *Daily Telegraph*
ran a competition to provide the best definition of
Englishness. This was the winning entry:

He views the Channel as a trench
Laughs at the Germans, hates the French
Though docile on his starchy diet
He'll rush abroad to quell a riot.
He hates a fuss, seldom complains
Accepts poor service and late trains.
But full of ale there's hell to pay –
Remember that on St George's Day.

The Englishman

St George he was for England,
And before he killed the dragon
He drank a pint of English ale
Out of an English flagon.
For though he fast right readily
In hair-shirt or in mail,
It isn't safe to give him cakes
Unless you give him ale.

St George he was for England,
And right gallantly set free
The lady left for dragon's meat
And tied up to a tree;
But since he stood for England
And knew what England means,
Unless you give him bacon
You mustn't give him beans.

St George he is for England,
And shall wear the shield he wore
When we go out in armour
With the battle-cross before.
But though he is jolly company
And very pleased to dine,
It isn't safe to give him nuts
Unless you give him wine.

G K Chesterton

We English Are So Great, We Don't Need to Tell You About It

Today, as most true Englishmen almost certainly won't be aware, is St George's Day and, like most true Englishmen, I'm not going to be celebrating it because we English don't go in for that sort of thing. We're aware that other countries like to set aside special days to paint themselves tartan or impersonate dragons or toast each other in poetic, but moribund, tongues and generally give themselves a big up for coming from somewhere obscure and ethnic. But we English, we don't need to. When you spend 365 days every year knowing how wonderful it is to have been born in the land that invented pretty much everything that is good, beautiful and noble, why single out one day for special treatment?

That's the way I look at it, but I must admit it wasn't always so. At school, I remember feeling terribly left out when we all gathered to watch rugger internationals. I seemed to be the only person who couldn't claim ancestral ties with the opposition. Wales, Scotland, Fernando Po, it didn't matter. The point, my school-mates sensed, was that to be English was to be allied with the forces of the quotidian, the naff and the bland.

Which is a notion that continues to be exploited by the marketing industry. Why else does every other pub in Britain now have signs saying *Cead Mille Failte* in the nooks where they used to hang hunting prints? How come almost every film about British yoof culture – *Trainspotting, Morvern Callar, Human Traffic* – is set in Wales or Scotland? Why is it that every St Patrick's Day thousands of Englishmen who wouldn't know what the craic was if they put it in a pipe and smoked it, paint their faces green, drink Guinness till their bottoms fall out and sing rebel songs written by the people who tried to blow up their grandparents?

St George himself gets a raw deal too. His flag (surely the world's chic-est, less-is-more-ist) is misrepresented as a jingoistic rag; his reputation has been traduced by revisionists who claim that he didn't really kill a dragon at all, it was a worm he speared with a toothpick, and anyway the worm was already half-dead.

But we don't need to allow the proselytising choppiness of those unfortunate enough not to have been born English to deceive us into thinking that we have anything to feel guilty or embarrassed about. I do hate to quote one of our patriotic drinking songs because patriotic drinking songs are so cheesy. But the minstrel didn't lie when he sang: 'The English, the English, the English are best.' Think about it: we invented practical democracy (Magna Carta, Parliament); the greatest language on the planet; English literature (Chaucer, Shakespeare, Milton, etc); popular culture (the Beatles); America (the Pilgrim Fathers, etc); the post-coital cigarette (Sir Walter Raleigh); Australia (convicts); suspension bridges, and probably lots of other cool sorts of bridges too, only I don't know about the subject (Brunel); recreational drug use (De Quincey); we ran the world's largest, richest and most benign empire; we produce its doughtiest explorers, its finest, most resourceful soldiers, sailors and airmen. And not for a moment am I suggesting that we managed all this without the help of the Welsh, Scottish and Irish because I have no need. Being English, one never has to feel chippy about anything.

And I haven't even got on to sport. We invented almost all the world's games: rugger, football, tennis, cricket, darts. Yet such is our modesty that, rather than hanging about, crowing about how good we are and dominating the field, we have generously allowed other, less inventive, nations to get better at these games than we are.

Truly, it's all I can do to stop a shy tear coursing down my cheek. But stop it I must, for it's only St George's Day — for an Englishman, a day like any other.

James Delingpole
The Times

The Other England

Behind 'the dark Satanic mills' that spoilt our native land,
Behind the dismal city streets where crowded houses stand,
There still lies another country that's grounded in the past,
Where rootless, city folk still dream they'll find true peace at
*   last.*

The beauty of our countryside beyond the urban sprawl,
Still holds a rich diversity to touch the hearts of all.
From the rugged border country, through northern dales and
*   fells,*
To the gentler, southern counties it weaves its magic spells.

*From 'England's Garden' in the east with rich and fertile
    ground,
To Cornwall with its storm-tossed cliffs where Celtic myths
    abound,
In countless, ancient villages another England lies
With church and inn and manor house whose witness still
    survives.
Our lovely countryside remains in spite of every threat,
To be cherished and protected, lest one day we forget
That it's deep in rural England that our roots are to be found
And the land we treat so lightly is really hallowed ground.*

*For beside the village churches with which our land is blest,
The bodies of our forefathers were gently laid to rest.
For all of us were country folk, until industrial change
Transformed the face of English towns and rural life grew
    strange.*

*Today St George, our Patron Saint, still flies the banner
    high,
The symbol of the land we love, its earth, its sea, its sky.
Like him we pray that we may stand in hamlet, village,
    town,
For this other land of England – our pride, our joy, our
    Crown!*

Canon E W Eyden

Breathes There The Man, With Soul So Dead?

What should they know of England,

Who only England know?

Rudyard Kipling

From The Lay of The Last Minstrel

Breathes there the man, with soul so dead,
Who never to himself hath said,
This is my own, my native land!
Whose heart hath ne'er within him burn'd,
As home his footsteps he hath turn'd,
From wandering on a foreign strand!
If such there breathe, go, mark him well;
For him no Minstrel raptures swell,
High though his titles, proud his name,
Boundless his wealth as wish can claim;
Despite those titles, power, and pelf,
The wretch, concentred all in self,
Living, shall forfeit fair renown,
And, doubly dying, shall go down
To the vile dust, from whence he sprung,
Unwept, unhonour'd, and unsung.

Sir Walter Scott

The Wanderer

Oh, English air is fresh and pure and English homes are
    bright;
But I must wander far away and set my course tonight.
The English breeze will stir the leaves, but I shall not be here
When Spring goes tripping coyly out and Summer crowns
    the year.

The Summer sounds I love so well I shall not hear again;
The merry children running free and shouting through the
    lane;
The liquid flutes of little birds and, melting in a dream,
The whisper of the swaying boughs, the murmur of the
    stream.
The waggons rumbling up the road, the droning of the bees,
The parliament of busy rooks that caw about the trees.
The air will fill with English songs, but I shall hear no more
Till God shall bid me steer for home and set me on the shore.

Oh, then I'll wander back again and seek the place I knew
When all the world was young and fair and all the tales were
    true.
And I may find a hand or two that keep a grip for me,
When I come back to English earth from tossing on the sea.

                                        Rudolph Chambers Lehmann

Home Thoughts From Abroad

Oh, to be in England
Now that April's there,
And whoever wakes in England
Sees, some morning, unaware,
That the lowest boughs and the brushwood sheaf
Round the elm-tree bole are in tiny leaf,
While the chaffinch sings on the orchard bough
In England – now!
And after April, when May follows,
And the whitethroat builds, and all the swallows!
Hark, where my blossomed pear-tree in the hedge
Leans to the field and scatters on the clover
Blossoms and dewdrops – at the bent spray's edge –
That's the wise thrush; he sings each song twice over,
Lest you should think he never could recapture
The first fine careless rapture!
And though the fields look rough with hoary dew
All will be gay when noontide wakes anew
The buttercups, the little children's dower
– Far brighter than this gaudy melon-flower!

Robert Browning

April 1986 was a particularly miserable month for
weather and it prompted this letter to *The Times*:

Home Thoughts

Sir,
Oh, not to be in England
    Now that April's there,
For whoever wakes in England
    Sees, each morning, in despair,
That the rain still rains,
    And the frost still freezes,
And Force 9 gales
    Are the soft Spring breezes;
(The elm-tree bole is Dutch-Elm-
                        dead)
And the hail clangs down
    On the potting shed,
    In England – now!
And after April, when May follows,
    I rather fear the only swallows
Will be from those who drown their
                        sorrows,
    Drained of hope of fine
                        tomorrows,
    In England – now!

John Stirling
Axbridge, Somerset

Ye Mariners of England

Ye Mariners of England
*   That guard our native seas!*
Whose flag has braved a thousand years
*   The battle and the breeze!*
Your glorious standard launch again
*   To match another foe;*
And sweep through the deep,
*   While the stormy winds do blow!*
While the battle rages loud and long
*   And the stormy winds do blow.*

The spirits of your fathers
*   Shall start from every wave –*
For the deck it was their field of fame,
*   And Ocean was their grave:*
Where Blake and mighty Nelson fell
*   Your manly hearts shall glow,*
As ye sweep through the deep,
While the stormy winds do blow!
While the battle rages loud and long
*   And the stormy winds do blow.*

Britannia needs no bulwarks,
    No towers along the steep;
Her march is o'er the mountain-waves,
    Her home is on the deep.
With thunders from her native oak
    She quells the floods below,
As they roar on the shore,
    When the stormy winds do blow!
When the battle rages loud and long,
    And the stormy winds do blow.

The meteor flag of England
    Shall yet terrific burn;
Till danger's troubled night depart
    And the star of peace return.
Then, then, ye ocean-warriors!
    Our song and feast shall flow
To the fame of your name,
    When the storm has ceased to blow!
When the fiery fight is heard no more,
    And the storm has ceased to blow.

Thomas Campbell

Sonnet Written in Mid-Channel

Austin demonstrates the sturdy patriotism that perhaps contributed to his selection as Poet Laureate, and would surely have pleased his contemporaries.

Now upon English soil I soon shall stand,
Homeward from climes that fancy deems more fair;
And well I know that there will greet me there
No soft foam fawning upon smiling strand,
No scent of orange-groves, no zephyrs bland,
But Amazonian March, with breast half bare
And sleety arrows whistling through the air,
Will be my welcome from that burly land.
Yet he who boasts his birthplace yonder lies,
Owns in his heart a mood akin to scorn
For sensuous slopes that bask 'neath Southern skies,
Teeming with wine, and prodigal of corn,
And, gazing through the mist with misty eyes,
Blesses the brave bleak land where he was born.

Alfred Austin

I Travelled Among Unknown Men

I travelled among unknown Men,
*   In Lands beyond the Sea;*
Nor England! did I know till then
*   What love I bore to thee.*

Tis past, that melancholy dream!
*   Nor will I quit thy shore*
A second time; for still I seem
*   To love thee more and more.*

Among thy mountains did I feel
*   The joy of my desire;*
And She I cherished turned her wheel
*   Beside an English fire.*

Thy mornings shewed – thy nights concealed
*   The bowers where Lucy played;*
And thine is, too, the last green field
*   Which Lucy's eyes surveyed!*

William Wordsworth

England . . . Home of the World

Hail to thee, England – Blest isle of the ocean,
Thy proud deeds awaken the fondest emotion,
Whose name shall forever live famous in story,
As the watchword of freedom, and birthplace of glory.

Thy sons ever brave, stay true to their duty,
Thy daughters are fair, lovely emblems of beauty,
The joys that surround our byways dew-pearled,
In England, old England . . . main home of the world.

Couch'd is her lion . . . Britannia reposes,
Encircled by laurels, amid her bright roses,
Her warriors at rest and her banners all furl'd
Hail to thee England! Sweet home of the world.

Ye who would rail 'gainst the land of the stranger,
Who would by disunion its blessings endanger,
Go search foreign climes for a country so glorious,
As England, old England, forever victorious!

Long may her Navy, triumphantly sailing,
And Army still conquer with courage unfailing,
Their thunder will forever 'gainst tyrants be hurl'd
Hail to thee, England! Dear home of the world.

From 'The Victorian Songster for 1839'
Anon

O England, Country of my Heart's Desire

O England, country of my heart's desire,
Land of the hedgerow and the village spire,
Land of thatched cottages and murmuring bees,
And wayside inns where one may take one's ease.
Of village green where cricket may be played
And fat old squirrels sleeping in the shade –
O Homeland, far across the main,
How I would love to see your face again! –
Your daisied meadows and your grassy hills,
Your primrose banks, your parks, your tinkling rills,
Your copses where the purple bluebells grow
Your quiet lanes where lovers linger so,
Your cottage-gardens with their wallflowers' scent,
Your swallows 'neath the eaves, your sweet content!
And 'mid the fleecy clouds that o'er you spread.
Listen, the skylark singing overhead –
    That's the old country, that's the old home!
    You never forget it wherever you roam.

E V Lucas

Tell England

Tell England . . . we shall soon come back
To the woods in bluebell time,
To see the dancing daffodils,
The chestnut and the lime,
To climb the purple heather hill
And find the cold wind blows there still . . .

Tell England . . . we shall never forget
Her Devon lanes, nor her Downs
In Sussex by an English sea,
And all her quaint old towns,
And London, peerless through the years,
With all her laughter and her tears . . .

Tell England . . . we shall soon come back
Weary and worn and lone,
Out of the heat of the land we serve
To the land that is our own.
Oh tell her, before the evening chime,
That we'll come back . . . in bluebell time!

Elizabeth Dunstan-Crarey

Home Thoughts from the Sea

Nobly, nobly Cape Saint Vincent
To the North-west died away;
Sunset ran, one glorious blood-red,
Reeking into Cadiz Bay;
Bluish 'mid the burning water,
Full in face Trafalgar lay;
In the dimmest North-east distance
Dawned Gibraltar grand and gray;
'Here and here did England help me;
How can I help England?' – say,
Whoso turns as I this evening,
Turn to God to praise and pray,
While Jove's planet rises yonder,
Silent over Africa.

Robert Browning

Sing a Song of England

The English may not like music,

But they absolutely love the noise it makes.

Sir Thomas Beecham

There'll Always Be An England

I give you a toast, ladies and gentlemen.
I give you a toast, ladies and gentlemen.
May this fair dear land we love so well
In dignity and freedom dwell.
Though worlds may change and go awry
While there is still one voice to cry –

There'll always be an England
While there's a country lane,
Wherever there's a cottage small
Beside a field of grain.
There'll always be an England
While there's a busy street,
Wherever there's a turning wheel,
A million marching feet.

Red, white and blue; what does it mean to you?
Surely you're proud, shout it aloud,
'Britons, awake!'
The empire too, we can depend on you.
Freedom remains. These are the chains
Nothing can break.

There'll always be an England,
And England shall be free
If England means as much to you
As England means to me.

Parker & Charles

We'll Gather Lilacs

Although you're far away
And life is sad and grey
I have a scheme, a dream to try
I'm thinking, dear of you
And all I mean to do
When we're together you and I
We'll soon forget our care and pain
And find such lovely things to share again.

Refrain:
We'll gather lilacs in the spring again
And walk together down an English lane
Until our hearts have learned to sing again
When you come home once more
And in the evening by the firelight's glow
You'll hold me close and never let me go.
Your eyes will tell me all I want to know
When you come home once more.

We'll learn to love anew
The simple joys we knew
And shared together night and day
We'll watch without a sigh
The moments speeding by
When life is free and hearts are gay
My dream is here for you to share
And in my heart my dream becomes a prayer.

Refrain.

Ivor Novello

Song of Patriotic Prejudice

The rottenest bits of these islands of ours
We've left in the hands of three unfriendly powers;
Examine the Irishman, Welshman or Scot,
You'll find he's a stinker as likely as not!
    The English, the English, the English are best!
    I wouldn't give tuppence for all of the rest!

The Scotsman is mean, as we're all well aware,
And bony and blotchy and covered with hair;
He eats salty porridge, he works all the day
And he hasn't got Bishops to show him the way.
    The English, the English, the English are best!
    I wouldn't give tuppence for all of the rest!

The Irishman now our contempt is beneath;
He sleeps in his boots, and he lies in his teeth;
He hates all the English, or so I have heard,
And blames it on Cromwell and William the Third.
    The English are noble, the English are nice,
    And worth any other at double the price!

The Welshman's dishonest – he cheats when he can –
And little and dark, more like monkey than man;
He works underground with a lamp in his hat
And sings far too loud, far too often, and flat.
  The English, the English, the English are best!
  I wouldn't give tuppence for all of the rest!

And crossing the Channel one cannot say much
For the French or the Spanish, the Danish or Dutch;
The Germans are German, the Russians are Red
And the Greeks and Italians eat garlic in bed.
  The English are moral, the English are good
  And clever and modest and misunderstood.

And all the world over each nation's the same –
They've simply no notion of Playing the Game;
They argue with Umpires, they cheer when they've won,
And they practise beforehand, which spoils all the fun!
  The English, the English, the English are best!
  So up with the English and down with the rest!

It's not that they're wicked or naturally bad:
It's knowing they're foreign that makes them so mad!
For the English are all that a nation should be
And the flower of the English are you, dear reader and me!
  The English, the English, the English are best!
  I wouldn't give tuppence for all of the rest!

Michael Flanders
Flanders & Swann

Glorious Devon

Coombe and Tor, green meadow and lane,
Birds on the waving bough,
Beetling cliffs by the surging main,
Rich red loam for the plough;
Devon's the fount of the bravest blood
That braces England's breed,
For maidens fair as the apple bud,
And her men are men indeed.

When Adam and Eve were dispossess'd
Of the Garden hard by Heaven,
They planted another one down in the West,
'Twas Devon, 'twas Devon, glorious Devon.

Spirits to old-world heroes wake,
By river and cove and hoe,
Grenville, Hawkins, Raleigh and Drake
    And a thousand more we know;
To ev'ry land the wide world o'er
Some slips of the old stock roam,
Leal friends in peace, dread foes in war,
With hearts still true to home.

Old England's counties by the sea
From East to West are seven,
But the gem of that fair galaxy
Is Devon, is Devon, glorious Devon.

Dorset, Somerset, Cornwall, Wales,
May envy the likes of we,
For the flow'r of the West, the first, the best,
The pick of the bunch us be;
Squab pie, junket, and cyder brew,
Richest of cream from the cow,
What 'ud Old England without 'em do?
And where 'ud 'un be to now?

As crumpy as a lump of lead
Be a loaf without good leaven,
And the yeast Mother England do use for her bread
Be Devon, be Devon, glorious Devon.

Sir Harold Boulton

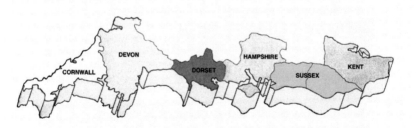

The Stately Homes of England

The Stately Homes of England, How beautiful they stand
To prove the upper classes still have the upper hand
Though the fact that they have to be rebuilt
And frequently mortgaged to the hilt
Is inclined to take the gilt
Off the gingerbread
And certainly damps the fun of the eldest son

But still we won't be beaten, We'll scrimp and screw and
*   save*
The playing fields of Eton, have made us frightfully brave
And though if the Van Dycks have to go
And we pawn the Bechstein Grand
We'll stand by the Stately Homes of England

The Stately Homes of England we proudly represent
We only keep them up for Americans to rent
Though the pipes that supply the bathroom burst
And the lavat'ry makes you fear the worst
It was used by Charles the First – quite informally
And later by George the Fourth
On a journey North

The State Apartments keep their historical renown
It's wiser not to sleep there in case they tumble down
But still if they ever catch on fire,
Which with any luck they might
We'll fight for the Stately Homes of England

The Stately Homes of England, though rather in the lurch
Provide a lot of chances for psychical research
There's the ghost of a crazy younger son
Who murdered in thirteen fifty-one
An extremely rowdy nun
Who resented it
And people who come to call, meet her in the hall

The baby in the guest wing who crouches by the grate
Was walled up in the West wing in fourteen twenty-eight
If anyone spots the Queen of Scots
In a hand embroidered shroud
We're proud of the Stately Homes of England

Noël Coward

HER MAJESTY AT CHATSWORTH.—THE GRAND ENTRANCE.—See page 575.

When glorious Anne became our Queen,
   The Church of England's glory,
Another face of things was seen,
   And I became a Tory:
Occasional Conformists base
   I damned, and Moderation,
And thought the Church in danger was
   From such prevarication.
      And this is Law, etc.

When George in pudding time came o'er,
   And moderate men looked big, Sir,
My principles I changed once more,
   And so became a Whig, Sir:
And thus preferment I procured
   From our Faith's Great Defender,
And almost every day abjured
   The Pope and the Pretender.
      And this is Law, etc.

The illustrious House of Hanover,
   And Protestant Succession,
To these I lustily will swear,
   Whilst they can keep possession:
For in my Faith and Loyalty
   I never once will falter,
But George my lawful King shall be,
   Except the times should alter.
      And this is Law, etc.

Anon

When two Englishmen meet their first talk is of
the weather.

Dr Johnson

The Englishman

He is an Englishman!
For he himself has said it,
And it's greatly to his credit,
That he is an Englishman!
For he might have been a Roosian,
A French, or Turk, or Proosian,
Or perhaps Itali-an!
But in spite of all temptations,
To belong to other nations,
He remains an Englishman!
Hurrah!
For the true-born Englishman!

From *HMS Pinafore* by W S Gilbert

Lord Byron described the English winter as
'ending in July – to begin again in August'.

Rose of England

Hear my voice and listen well, and a story I will tell,
How duty brought a broken heart, and why a love so strong
Must fall apart;

She was lovely, she was fine, daughter of a royal line,
He, no equal, but for them it mattered little for they were in
*   love;*

Rose of England, sweet and fair, shining with the sun,
Rose of England, have a care, for where the thorn is,
There the blood will run;

Oh my heart, oh my heart;

Through the summer days and nights, stolen kisses and
*   delights*
Would thrill their hearts and fill their dreams with all
*   emotions*
That true love can bring;

But black of mourning came one day, when her sister passed
*   away,*
And many said on bended knee, she has gone, and you must
*   be our Queen;*

Rose of England, sweet and fair, shining with the sun,
Rose of England, have a care, for where the thorn is,
There the blood will run;

Oh my heart, oh my heart;

To the abbey she did ride, with her lover by her side,
When they heard the church bells ring, she was Queen
And one day, he'd be King;

But men of malice, men of hate, protesting to her chambers
  came,
'A foreign prince will have your hand, for he'll bring peace
And riches to our land;'
She said, 'Do you tell me that I cannot wed the one I love?
Do you tell me that I am not mistress of my heart?'
And so with heavy weight of life she kissed her lover one last
  time,
'This land I wed, and no man comes, for if I cannot have you,
  I'll have none;'

Rose of England, sweet and fair, shining with the sun,
Rose of England have a care, for where the thorn is,
There the blood will run;

Oh my heart, oh my heart.

Written by Chris de Burgh
From *The Road to Freedom*

There grows the flower of Peace
The Rose that cannot wither.

From *Silex Scintillans, Peace*
Henry Vaughan

Rose of England

Grown in one land alone,
Where proud winds have blown;
There's not a flow'r
Born of the show'r
Braver than England's own.

Though gales of winter blow
Piercing hail and snow,
Shining she stays,
Bright as in days of yore,

Old England's pride still blossoms
fresh on England's shore.

Refrain:
Rose of England, thou shalt fade not here,
Proud and bright from rolling year to year.
Red shall thy petals be as rich wine untold
Shed by thy warriors who served thee of old.

Rose of England, breathing England's air,
Flower of Liberty beyond compare;
While hand and heart endure to cherish thy
   prime,
Thou shalt blossom to the end of Time.

Christopher Hassall

Greensleeves

Alas! my love, you do me wrong
To cast me off discourteously;
And I have loved you so long,
Delighting in your company.

Greensleeves was all my joy!
Greensleeves was my delight!
Greensleeves was my heart of gold!
And who but my Lady Greensleeves!

I bought thee petticoats of the best,
The cloth so fine as fine as might be;
I gave thee jewels for thy chest,
And all this cost I spent on thee.

Thy smock of silk, both fair and white,
With gold embroidered gorgeously;
Thy petticoat of sendal right:
And these I bought thee gladly.

Thy gown was of the grassy green,
The sleeves of satin hanging by;
Which made thee be our harvest queen:
And yet thou wouldest not love me!

Greensleeves now farewell! adieu!
God I pray to prosper thee!
For I am still thy lover true:
Come once again and love me!

Greensleeves was all my joy!
Greensleeves was my delight!
Greensleeves was my heart of gold!
And who but my Lady Greensleeves!

Anon

The White Cliffs of Dover

I'll never forget the people I met
Braving those angry skies
I remember well as the shadows fell
The light of hope in their eyes
And though I'm far away
I still hear them say
Thumbs Up!!
For when the dawn comes up . . .

There'll be blue birds over
The white cliffs of Dover,
Tomorrow, just you wait and see.

There'll be love and laughter
And peace ever after
Tomorrow, when the world is free.

I may not be near But I have no fear
Hist'ry will prove it too
When the tale is told, 'Twill be as of old
For truth will always win through
But be I far or near
That slogan still I'll hear,
Thumbs Up!!
For when the dawn comes up . . .

The shepherd will tend his sheep,
The valley will bloom again
And Jimmy will go to sleep,
In his own little room again.

There'll be blue birds over
The white cliffs of Dover,
Tomorrow, just you wait and see.

Nat Burton

It's Almost Tomorrow

It's almost tomorrow,
No longer today,
An hour that is timeless,
The right time to say
A sentimental goodbye to you,
No sorrow, tomorrow's in view.
It's almost tomorrow
And soon we must part,
Another new morning,
Another new start,
But now it's time to go on our way
And dream of tomorrow today.

Go on your way, on your way, on your way...

Finale of *Joyce Grenfell Requests The Pleasure*
Joyce Grenfell

O Peaceful England

O Peaceful England, While I my watch am keeping
Thou, like Minerva, weary of war, art sleeping
Sleep on a little while, And in thy slumber smile
While thou art sleeping, I'll be wakeful, ever wakeful

 Sword and buckler by thy side
 Rest on the shore of battletide
 Which like the ever hungry sea,
 Howls round this isle
 O sleep 'til I awaken thee
 And in thy slumber, smile

England, fair England, Well hast thou earned thy slumber
Yet though thy bosom no breastplate now encumber
Let not thy fingers yield Grasp of thy sword and shield
Thou shalt awake and wield Destruction when I call thee

 Sword and buckler by thy side . . .

From *Merrie England*
Edward German

The English Rose, from Merrie England

Dan Cupid hath a garden
Where women are the flow'rs
And lovers laughs and lovers tears
The sunshine and the show'rs
And Oh! the sweetest blossom
That in the garden grows
The fairest Queen, it is, I ween,
The perfect English Rose

Let others make a garland
Of ev'ry flow'r that blows
But I will wait till I may pluck
My dainty English Rose
In perfume, grace and beauty
The Rose doth stand apart
God grant that I, before I die
May wear one on my heart

Edward German

Our England is a Garden

A garden is a lovesome thing, God wot!

Thomas Edward Brown

The Glory of the Garden

Our England is a garden that is full of stately views,
Of borders, beds and shrubberies and lawns and avenues,
With statues on the terraces and peacocks strutting by;
But the Glory of the Garden lies in more than meets the eye.

For where the old thick laurels grow, along the thin red wall,
You find the tool- and potting-sheds which are the heart of
    all;
The cold-frames and the hot-houses, the dungpits and the
    tanks,
The rollers, carts and drain-pipes, with the barrows and the
    planks.

And there you'll see the gardeners, the men and 'prentice
    boys
Told off to do as they are bid and do it without noise;
For, except when seeds are planted and we shout to scare the
    birds,
The Glory of the Garden it abideth not in words.

And some can pot begonias and some can bud a rose,
And some are hardly fit to trust with anything that grows;
But they can roll and trim the lawns and sift the sand and
    loam,
For the Glory of the Garden occupieth all who come.

Our England is a garden, and such gardens are not made
By singing: – 'Oh, how beautiful!' and sitting in the shade,
While better men than we go out and start their working
    lives
At grubbing weeds from gravel-paths with broken dinner-
    knives.

There's not a pair of legs so thin, there's not a head so thick,
There's not a hand so weak and white, nor yet a heart so sick,
But it can find some needful job that's crying to be done,
For the Glory of the Garden glorifieth every one.

Then seek your job with thankfulness and work till further
    orders,
If it's only netting strawberries or killing slugs on borders;
And when your back stops aching and your hands begin to
    harden,
You will find yourself a partner in the Glory of the Garden.

Oh, Adam was a gardener, and God who made him sees
That half a proper gardener's work is done upon his knees,
So when your work is finished, you can wash your hands and
    pray
For the Glory of the Garden, that it may not pass away!
And the Glory of the Garden it shall never pass away!

                                        Rudyard Kipling

English Country Gardens

How many kinds of sweet flowers grow
In an English country garden?
We'll tell you now of some that we know
Those we miss you'll surely pardon
Daffodils, heart's ease and flox
Meadowsweet and lady smocks
Gentian, lupine and tall hollyhocks
Roses, foxgloves, snowdrops, blue forget-me-nots
In an English country garden.

How many insects come here and go
In an English country garden?
We'll tell you now of some that we know
Those we miss you'll surely pardon
Fireflies, moths, gnats and bees
Spiders climbing in the trees
Butterflies drift in the gentle breeze
There are snakes, ants that sting
And other creeping things
In an English country garden.

How many songbirds fly to and fro
In an English country garden?
We'll tell you now of some that we know
Those we miss you'll surely pardon
Bobolink, cuckoo and quail
Tanager and cardinal
Bluebird, lark, thrush and nightingale
There is joy in the spring
When the birds begin to sing
In an English country garden.

Traditional

I Leave My Heart In An English Garden

I leave my heart in an English Garden,
Safe where the elm and the oak stand by.
Tho' the years rise and roll away
Still shall those watchmen stay,
Bold in the blue of an English sky.

Breezes in the long grass ruffling my hair,
Hollyhock and bluebell scenting the air,
Nothing in the world can ever be
Such a sweet memory:
Nothing in the world was ever so fair.

I leave my dreams in an English garden,
Safe where the breezes of England blow.
When the highways are dark and drear,
I'll know there's sunshine here,
Bright where the roses of England grow.

Dawn on the Aegean redd'ning the foam,
Sunset over Cyprus, springtime in Rome.
Lovely are the lands where, I dare say,
I could stay for a day . . .
But none of them are quite as lovely as home.

Christopher Hassall

God's Garden

The Lord God planted a garden
In the first white days of the world,
And He set there an angel warden
In a garment of light enfurled.

So near to the peace of Heaven
The hawk might nest with the wren,
For there in the cool of the even
God walked with the first of men.

And I dream that these garden closes,
With their glades and their sun-flecked sod,
And their lilies and bowers of roses,
Were laid by the hand of God.

The kiss of the sun for pardon,
The song of the birds for mirth,
One is nearer God's heart in a garden,
Than anywhere else on earth.

The dawn of the morn for glory,
The hush of the night for peace,
In the garden at eve, says the story,
God walks, and His smile brings release.

Dorothy Frances Gurney

That Which We Call a Rose

Flower of liberty beyond compare

On the Rose

What sweeter flower in England but the rose
Brings colour and perfume to summer days,
Providing themes for poetry and prose,
For music, painting, literature and plays.
Where would the rival Northern counties be
Without their old symbolic red and white,
Plantagenet and Tudor dynasty,
The rose, an emblem of their Divine Right?

A thornless rose the Virgin doth portray,
To demonstrate her life of purity,
While Venus with a thorned rose doth play,
To show the wounds of love, with Graces three.
A metaphor for beauty, grace and love,
Surely this flower will bloom in Heaven above.

Sheila Arnoldi

Roses

You love the roses – so do I. I wish
The sky would rain down roses, as they rain
From off the shaken bush. Why will it not?
Then all the valley would be pink and white
And soft to tread on. They would fall as light
As feathers, smelling sweet: and it would be
Like sleeping and yet waking, all at once.

George Eliot

Look to the blowing Rose about us.
'Lo, laughing,' she says, 'into the world I blow:
At once the silken tassel of my purse tear,
And its treasure on the garden throw.

From the Rubaiyat of Omar Khayyam

Unkempt about those hedges blows
An English unofficial rose.

The Old Vicarage, Grantchester
Rupert Brooke

The Wars of the Roses

The single event that could be said to have started the Wars of the Roses happened in 1399. Henry Bolingbroke seized the throne from Edward III's grandson Richard II and declared himself King Henry IV. Henry attacked Richard physically, claiming the right of trial by combat. Richard put up no resistance and disappeared, imprisoned by the new king shortly afterwards. Although Richard was a weak king, the people opposed Henry until his death. His son, crowned Henry V, proved to be a great king. He restored the country's faith in the monarchy with his victories in France. Some never forgot, though, how their own lineage had been severed by the rise of these usurper kings from the house of Lancaster.

Henry V died suddenly in 1422, leaving the one-year-old Prince Henry as heir. Henry VI was an ineffectual king, unpopular with his people because he listened too much to his current favourite advisers – out for personal gain – and his wife, the unpopular and domineering Margaret of Anjou. A string of bad decisions angered Richard, Duke of York, whom many people believed to have a legitimate claim to the throne himself. He was seen as a threat by those close to the king, so was called back from his important post in Calais and effectually banished to Ireland. This seems to have been the last straw for Richard, who had supported the king completely until that point. It was then that the Wars of the Roses truly started, with Richard, a plausible heir to the throne, seeking the crown for himself. He never gained it; but his son, Edward IV, took the kingdom from Henry in 1471.

A few months after his coronation, Henry once more regained the throne. He held it for only a few months and then Edward captured Henry and seized power for himself again. All was quiet for eleven years, until in 1483 Edward IV died. He left his two young sons Edward and Richard in the care of their uncle, Richard of York. Both boys vanished (presumed killed in the Tower of London) and Richard pronounced himself King of England. In 1485, however, another claimant to the throne, Henry Tudor, landed in England and marched across the country. He gathered support for his claim to the throne by his Lancastrian ancestry. On 22 August 1485 Richard and Henry met at Bosworth. By the end of the day, Henry was crowned King of England, and Richard was dead.

Henry was opposed by only a few remaining lords and nobles. These were either with him or dead by 1490. With his marriage to the last of the Yorkist line, the Wars of the Roses could be said to be finally over.

Lancaster   York

That Which We Call a Rose

According to a minor Latin poet, the rose was born from a smile of Cupid, a proposition not difficult to accept. Oh, happy smile that could give birth to the enormous pleasure contained in that flower we know as the rose.

'What's in a name?' asked Shakespeare. 'That which we call a rose, by any other name would smell as sweet.' Well, up to a point. True, a change of name would not alter the fragrance of this 'flower of liberty beyond compare' – by any other name it would still pleasure us and delight our senses to provide what Milton was pleased to call 'a steam of rich distilled perfumes'. But we have to be careful of that 'any other name' bit. Botanists have now decided that the rose is genetically a member of the *Urtica* family, so it could have been called a nettle.

Let us suppose, though, that whichever Roman chose the name of this Queen of Flowers and Flower of Queens, unaware of its DNA connection with the nettle, had instead named it, say Antirrhinum or Snapdragon; while its ability to please our optical and olfactory senses would be undiminished, one cannot but wonder what effect it might have had on our perception of the flower generally. What would it do to our literature? What would it do to poetry and song? And in particular, what would it do to the *Oxford Book of Quotations*? Out would go about 150 references under the letter 'r'. Is it likely that the letter 'a', (which at present contains not a single reference to the antirrhinum), would swell to a similar number? Hardly!

And what would it do for romance? (Rose is, after all, an anagram of Eros.) Is it possible that Juliet might say 'An antirrhinum by any other name would be easier to spell'? Would Petruchio woo Katherina by declaring her looks to be 'as clear as morning antirrhinums newly washed with dew'? – (and is the plural of antirrhinum, antirrhina? – Latin scholars please advise).

Patriotism would suffer, too. 'Antirrhinum of England, thou shall fade not here' doesn't have quite the same noble ring about it. Can you really imagine history students learning how the Lancastrian and Yorkist camps fought the Wars of the Antirrhinums? And what of York Minster? After the fire of 1984 that destroyed so much of the South Transept, would the authorities have been quite as keen to rebuild so painstakingly the 17,000 pieces of medieval glass, if it had been called the antirrhinum window?

That rich body of poetry devoted to the rose is just not substitutable by the A-word. Robbie Burns would never have dipped his quill to pen the lines 'O my luve's like a red, red antirrhinum', and nor would Herrick have urged us to 'Gather ye antirrhinum-buds while ye may'. How sad, too, to think that we would have been deprived of a delicious example of Dorothy Parker's acerbic wit if she had been forced to consider 'One perfect antirrhinum'.

On the other hand, William Blake, in one of his more despondent moments, might well have written 'O Antirrhinum thou art Sick'; the poor flower might have lost the will to live once it discovered it had been misnamed as a member of the Scrophulariaceous family. Our song cycle would be several spokes short of a wheel without the rose. Quite apart from our view of the adored young lady of Tralee, and the revised picture of the floral scene in Picardy, it is stretching credulity to its limits to imagine Barbra Streisand announcing that she was 'second-hand Anti-you-know-what'. And polished professional though he may have been, it is difficult to believe that Nelson Eddy could have kept a straight face as he looked deep into Jeanette Macdonald's eyes, and sang, 'Oh Antirrhinum-Marie, I love you'.

When it comes to naming our offspring, the change of name for our favourite flower would have a profound effect on the table listing the top twenty most popular names for girls. Had I ever met the Royal National Rose Society's revered patron, Queen Elizabeth, the Queen Mother, I don't think I would have bothered asking Her Majesty if she and the Duke of York had ever contemplated naming their beloved second daughter Margaret Antirrhinum – the answer would have been obvious.

No, Mr Shakespeare, you got this one wrong. As Master Montague and Miss Capulet discovered to their cost, the name does matter. Of course, it could be that the Great Man never actually wrote those words. There is a considerable body of opinion that is convinced that the Bard's great works were the product of someone else's pen. (I myself subscribe to the view that the plays were not written by William Shakespeare, but by another chap who happened to have the same name).

But what if the 16th-century author of those 150 sonnets and 37 plays (many of which we may assume were performed at the Antirrhinum Theatre on Bankside), did have a different name? Does it really matter? After all, as a wise man once wrote, 'What's in a name?'

Gerry Hanson

The Rose

According to a legend from the middle ages, the first roses appeared by miracle in Bethlehem as a result of the prayers of an innocent maiden who had been falsely accused and sentenced to death by burning at the stake. It is said that the fire failed to touch her and from the stakes grew roses.

In Christian symbolism the rose is emblematic of purity and represents a paragon, and is particularly applied to the Virgin Mary, who carries the title, 'Mystic Rose'.

The Tudor Rose

The rose is the national flower of England. When Henry of Richmond, son of Edmund Tudor, Earl of Richmond, became head of the House of Lancaster after the death of Henry VI in 1471, he adopted the red rose to emphasise his Lancastrian claims. After his victory at Bosworth in 1485 he became king as Henry VII. Following his marriage to Princess Elizabeth of York in 1486, the union of the two Houses produced the Tudor rose, a supra-imposition of the white rose on the red.

To Paint a Rose

There is nothing more difficult for a truly creative painter than to paint a rose because before he can do so, he has first to forget all the roses that were ever painted.

Henri Matisse

My Country, 'Tis of Thee

Let us now praise famous men

National Anthem

GOD save our gracious Queen,
Long live our noble Queen,
    God save the Queen!
Send her victorious,
Happy and glorious,
Long to reign over us,
    God save the Queen!

Thy choicest gifts in store
On her be pleased to pour,
    Long may she reign:
May she defend our laws,
And ever give us cause
To sing with heart and voice
    God save the Queen!

 Nor on this land alone,
But be God's mercies known
    From shore to shore:
Lord, make the nations see
That men should brothers be,
And form one family
    The wide world o'er.

Verses 1 and 2 Anon
Verse 3 W E Hickson

The noble kind of patriotism ... aims at ends that are worthy
of the whole of mankind.

Albert Schweitzer

Rejoice, O land, in God your Lord,
obey his will and keep his word;
for you the saints lift up their voice:
fear not, O land, in God rejoice!

Glad shall you be, with blessing crowned,
and joy and peace shall clothe you round;
yes, love with you shall make a home
until you see God's kingdom come.

He shall forgive your sins untold –
remember now his love of old;
walk in his way, his word adore,
and keep his truth for evermore.

Robert Bridges

Jerusalem

And did those feet in ancient time
Walk upon England's mountains green?
And was the holy Lamb of God
On England's pleasant pastures seen?

And did the Countenance Divine
Shine forth upon our clouded hills?
And was Jerusalem builded here
Among these dark Satanic Mills?

Bring me my Bow of burning gold!
Bring me my Arrows of desire!
Bring me my Spear! O clouds, unfold!
Bring me my Chariot of fire!

I will not cease from Mental Fight,
Nor shall my Sword sleep in my hand,
Till we have built Jerusalem
In England's green and pleasant land.

William Blake

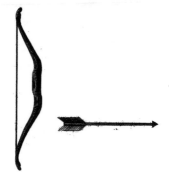

O Valiant Hearts

O valiant hearts, who to your glory came
Through dust of conflict and through battle flame;
Tranquil you lie, your knightly virtue proved,
Your memory hallowed in the land you loved.

Long years ago, as earth lay dark and still,
Rose a loud cry upon a lonely hill,
While in the frailty of our human clay,
Christ, our redeemer, passed the self-same way.

Proudly you gathered, rank on rank, to war,
As who had heard God's message from afar;
All you had hoped for, all you had, you gave,
To save mankind – yourself you scorned to save.

O risen Lord, O shepherd of our dead,
Whose cross has brought them and whose staff has led,
In glorious hope their proud and sorrowing land,
Commits her children to thy gracious hand.

Sir John S Arkwright

I Vow To Thee, My Country

I vow to thee, my country – all earthly things above –
Entire and whole and perfect, the service of my love:
The love that asks no question, the love that stands the test,
That lays upon the altar the dearest and the best;
The love that never falters, the love that pays the price,
The love that makes undaunted the final sacrifice.

And there's another country, I've heard of long ago,
Most dear to them that love her, most great to them that
     know;
We may not count her armies, we may not see her King;
Her fortress is a faithful heart, her pride is suffering;
And soul by soul and silently her shining bounds increase,
And her ways are ways of gentleness and all her paths are
     Peace.

Cecil Spring-Rice

Land of Hope and Glory

Dear Land of Hope, thy hope is crowned,
God make thee mightier yet!
On Sov'ran brows, beloved, renowned,
Once more thy crown is set.
Thine equal laws, by Freedom gained,
Have ruled thee well and long;
By Freedom gained, by Truth maintained,
Thine Empire shall be strong.

Land of Hope and Glory,
Mother of the Free,
How shall we extol thee,
Who are born of thee?
Wider still and wider shall thy bounds be set;
God, who made thee mighty, make thee mightier yet;
God, who made thee mighty, make thee mightier yet.

Thy fame is ancient as the days,
As Ocean large and wide;
A pride that dares, and heeds not praise,
A stern and silent pride;
Not that false joy that dreams content
With what our sires have won;
The blood a hero sire hath spent
Still nerves a hero son.

Land of Hope and Glory, etc.

Arthur C Benson

But When the Blast of War Blows In Our Ears ...

Give peace in our time, O Lord,
Because there is none other that fighteth for us,
But only thou, O God.

Book of Common Prayer

Henry V, Act III, Scene i

Once more unto the breach, dear friends, once more,
Or close the wall up with our English dead!
In peace there's nothing so becomes a man
As modest stillness and humility:
But when the blast of war blows in our ears,
Then imitate the action of the tiger;
Stiffen the sinews, conjure up the blood,
Disguise fair nature with hard-
    favoured rage;

                    Then lend the eye a
                    terrible aspect;
                    Let it pry through the
                    portage of the head
                    Like the brass cannon; let the
                    brow o'erwhelm it
                    As fearfully as doth a gallèd rock

O'erhang and jutty his confounded base,
Swilled with the wild and wasteful ocean.
Now set the teeth, and stretch the nostril wide,
Hold hard the breath, and bend up every spirit
To his full height! On, on, you noblest English,
Whose blood is fet from fathers of war-proof! –
Fathers that, like so many Alexanders,
Have in these parts from morn till even fought,
And sheathed their swords for lack of argument.
Dishonour not your mothers; now attest
That those whom you called fathers did beget you!
Be copy now to men of grosser blood,
And teach them how to war. And you, good yeomen,
Whose limbs were made in England, show us here
The mettle of your pasture; let us swear
That you are worth your breeding; which I doubt not;
For there is none of you so mean and base
That hath not noble lustre in your eyes.
I see you stand like greyhounds in the slips,
Straining upon the start. The game's afoot!
Follow your spirit, and upon this charge
Cry, 'God for Harry, England, and Saint George!'

William Shakespeare

Queen Elizabeth I's speech to her troops at Tilbury as they prepared to defend their country from the approaching Armada

My loving people, I am come amongst you, as you see, at this time, not for my recreation and disport, but being resolved, in the midst and heat of battle, to live or die amongst you all, to lay down for my God, and for my kingdom, and for my people, my honour and my blood, even in the dust. I know I have the body of a weak and feeble woman, but I have the heart and stomach of a king, and a king of England too, and I think foul scorn that Parma or Spain, or any prince of Europe should dare to invade the borders of my realm; to which, rather than any dishonour shall grow by me, I myself will take up arms, I myself will be your general, judge and rewarder of every one of your virtues in the field. I know, already for your forwardness you have deserved rewards and crowns; and we do assure you, in the word of a prince, they shall be duly paid you.

The Ironmonger's Grace

This is an Elizabethan Grace written in 1565 by George Belkin, ironmonger of Exeter.

God bless our meat
God guide our ways
God give us grace
Our Lord to please
Lord long preserve in peace and health
Our gracious Queen Elizabeth.

Drake's Drum

Drake he's in his hammock an' a thousand mile away,
  (Capten, art tha sleepin' there below?),
Slung atween the round shot in Nombre Dios Bay,
  An' dreamin' arl the time o' Plymouth Hoe.
Yarnder lumes the Island, yarnder lie the ships,
  Wi' sailor lads a dancin' heel-an'-toe,
An' the shore-lights flashin', an' the night-tide dashin',
  He sees et arl so plainly as he saw et long ago.

Drake he was a Devon man, an' rüled the Devon seas,
  (Capten, art tha sleepin' there below?),
Rovin' tho' his death fell, he went wi' heart at ease,
  An' dreamin' arl the time o' Plymouth Hoe.
'Take my drum to England, hang et by the shore,
  Strike et when your powder's runnin' low;
If the Dons sight Devon, I'll quit the port o'Heaven,
  An' drum them up the Channel as we drummed them long
    ago.'

Drake he's in his hammock till the great Armadas come,
  (Capten, art tha sleepin' there below?),
Slung atween the round shot, listenin' for the drum,
  An' dreamin' arl the time o' Plymouth Hoe.
Call him on the deep sea, call him up the Sound,
  Call him when ye sail to meet the foe;
Where the old trade's plyin' an' the old flag flyin'
They shall find him ware an' wakin', as they found him long
    ago!

Henry Newbolt

Song of the English Bowmen

Agincourt, Agincourt!
Know ye not Agincourt,
Where English slew and hurt
All their French foemen?
With their pikes and bills brown,
How the French were beat down,
Shot by our Bowmen!

Agincourt, Agincourt!
Know ye not Agincourt,
Never to be forgot,
Or known to no men?
Where English cloth-yard Arrows,
Killed the French like tame sparrows,
Slain by our Bowmen!

Agincourt, Agincourt!
Know ye not Agincourt,
English of every sort,
High men and low men,
Fought that day wondrous well,
All our old stories tell,
Thanks to our Bowmen!

Agincourt, Agincourt!
Know ye not Agincourt?
Where our fifth Harry taught
Frenchmen to know men:
And when the day was done,
Thousands fell to one
Good English Bowman!

Agincourt, Agincourt!
Know ye not Agincourt?
Dear was the victory bought
*   By fifty yeomen*
Ask any English wench,
They were worth all the French:
Rare English Bowmen!

Anon

The Other Little Boats

A pause came in the fighting and England held her breath
For the battle was not ended and the ending might be death,
Then out they came, the little boats, from all the Channel
  shores
Free men were those who set the sails and laboured at the
  oars.
From Itchenor and Shoreham, from Deal and Winchelsea,
They put out into the Channel to keep their country free.

Not of Dunkirk this story, but of boatmen long ago,
When our Queen was Gloriana and King Philip was our foe,
And galleons rode the Narrow Seas, and Effingham and
  Drake
Were out of shot and powder, with all England still at stake.

They got the shot and powder, they charged the guns again,
The guns that guarded England from the galleons of Spain,
And the men that helped them do it, helped them still to hold
  the sea
Men from Itchenor and Shoreham, men from Deal and
  Winchelsea,
Looked out happily from Heaven and cheered to see the work
Of their grandsons' grandsons' grandsons on the beaches of
  Dunkirk.

Edward Shanks

A Wet Sheet and a Flowing Sea

A wet sheet and a flowing sea,
*   A wind that follows fast*
And fills the white and rustling sail
*   And bends the gallant mast;*
And bends the gallant mast, my boys,
*   While like the eagle free*
Away the good ship flies and leaves
*   Old England on the lee.*

O for a soft and gentle wind!
*   I heard a fair one cry;*
But give to me that snoring breeze
*   And white waves heaving high;*
And white waves heaving high, my lads,
*   The good ship tight and free –*
The world of waters is our home,
*   And merry men are we.*

There's tempest in yon hornèd moon,
*   And lightning in yon cloud;*
But hark the music, mariners!
*   The wind is piping loud;*
The wind is piping loud, my boys,
*   The lightning flashes free –*
While the hollow oak our palace is,
*   Our heritage the sea.*

Allan Cunningham

Dover Beach

The sea is calm to-night.
The tide is full, the moon lies fair
Upon the straits; – on the French coast, the light
Gleams, and is gone; the cliffs of England stand,
Glimmering and vast, out in the tranquil bay.
Come to the window, sweet is the night-air!
Only, from the lone line of spray
Where the sea meets the moon-blanch'd sand,
Listen! you hear the grating roar
Of pebbles which the waves draw back, and fling,
At their return, up the high strand,
Begin, and cease, and then again begin,
With tremulous cadence slow, and bring
The eternal note of sadness in.

Sophocles long ago
Heard it on the Ægæan, and it brought
Into his mind the turbid ebb and flow
Of human misery; we
Find also in the sound a thought,
Hearing it by this distant northern sea.

The Sea of Faith
Was once, too, at the full, and round earth's shore
Lay like the folds of a bright girdle furl'd.
But now I only hear
Its melancholy, long, withdrawing roar,
Retreating, to the breath
Of the night-wind down the vast edges drear
And naked shingles of the world.

Ah, love, let us be true
To one another! for the world, which seems
To lie before us like a land of dreams,
So various, so beautiful, so new,
Hath really neither joy, nor love, nor light,
Nor certitude, nor peace, nor help for pain;
And we are here as on a darkling plain
Swept with confused alarms of struggle and flight,
Where ignorant armies clash by night.

Matthew Arnold

To Lucasta, Going to the Wars

Tell me not, sweet, I am unkind,
*   That from the nunnery*
Of thy chaste breast and quiet mind,
*   To war and arms I fly.*

True, a new mistress now I chase,
*   The first foe in the field;*
And with a stronger faith embrace
*   A sword, a horse, a shield.*

Yet this inconstancy is such
*   As you too shall adore;*
I could not love thee, dear, so much,
*   Lov'd I not Honour more.*

Richard Lovelace

The Rumour

Actual evidence, I have none
But my Aunt's charwoman's sister's son
Heard a policeman on his beat
Say to a housemaid in Downing Street
That he had a brother who had a friend
Who knew when the war was going to end.

A Soldier Stood at the Pearly Gate

A soldier stood at the pearly gate
His face was scarred and old.
He stood before the man of fate
For admission to the fold.

'What have you done,' St Peter asked,
'To gain admission here?'
'I've been a soldier, sir,' he said
'For many and many a year.'

The pearly gate swung open wide
As Peter touched the bell
'Inside', he said, 'and choose your harp
You've had your share of hell.'

Anon

We don't want to fight but, by jingo, if we do
We've got the ships, we've got the men, we've got
the money too.

G W Hunt
Music hall song

Lie In the Dark and Listen

Lie in the dark and listen
It's clear tonight so they're flying high
Hundreds of them, thousands perhaps
Riding the icy, moonlit sky
Men, machinery, bombs and maps
Altimeters and guns and charts
Coffee, sandwiches, fleece-lined boots
Bones and muscles and minds and hearts
English saplings with English roots
Deep in the earth they've left below
Lie in the dark and let them go
Lie in the dark and listen.

Lie in the dark and listen
They're going over in waves and waves
High above villages, hills and streams,
Country churches and little graves
And little citizens' worried dreams
Very soon they'll have reached the sea
And far below them will lie the bays
And cliffs and sands where they used to be
Taken for summer holidays
Lie in the dark and let them go
Theirs is a world we'll never know
Lie in the dark and listen.

Lie in the dark and listen
City magnates and steel contractors
Factory workers and politicians
Soft hysterical little actors
Ballet dancers, reserved musicians
Safe in your warm civilian beds
Count your profits and count your sheep
Life is passing over your heads

Just turn over and try to sleep
Lie in the dark and let them go
There's one debt you'll forever owe
Lie in the dark and listen.

Noël Coward

Courage, brother! do not stumble,
Though thy path is dark as night;
There's a star to guide the humble;
Trust in God, and do the Right.

Norman Macleod

In Westminster Abbey

Let me take this other glove off
  As the vox humana *swells,*
And the beauteous fields of Eden
  Bask beneath the Abbey bells.
Here, where England's statesmen lie,
Listen to a lady's cry.

Gracious Lord, oh bomb the Germans.
  Spare their women for Thy Sake,
And if that is not too easy
  We will pardon Thy Mistake.
But, gracious Lord, whate'er shall be,
Don't let anyone bomb me.

Keep our Empire undismembered
  Guide our Forces by Thy Hand,
Gallant blacks from far Jamaica,
  Honduras and Togoland;
Protect them Lord in all their fights,
And, even more, protect the whites.

Think of what our Nation stands for,
Books from Boots' and country lanes,
Free speech, free passes, class distinction,
Democracy and proper drains.
Lord, put beneath Thy special care
One-eighty-nine Cadogan Square.

Although dear Lord I am a sinner,
I have done no major crime;
Now I'll come to Evening Service
Whensoever I have the time.
So, Lord, reserve for me a crown,
And do not let my shares go down.

I will labour for Thy Kingdom,
Help our lads to win the war,
Send white feathers to the cowards
Join the Women's Army Corps,
Then wash the Steps around Thy Throne
In the Eternal Safety Zone.

Now I feel a little better,
What a treat to hear Thy Word,
Where the bones of leading statesmen,
Have so often been interr'd.
And now, dear Lord, I cannot wait
Because I have a luncheon date.

John Betjeman

As an example of typical English phlegm it would be hard to beat the temporary rules introduced in 1940 by the Richmond Golf Club.

'In competition, during gunfire, or while bombs are falling, players may take cover without penalty for ceasing play. The positions of known delayed-action bombs are marked by a red flag at a reasonably, but not guaranteed, safe distance therefrom. A ball moved by enemy action, or, if lost or destroyed, a ball may be dropped not nearer the hole without a penalty. A player whose stroke is affected by the simultaneous explosion of a bomb may play another ball from the same place. Penalty, one stroke.'

Soldiers

Soldiers who wish to be a hero
Are practically zero,
But those who wish to be civilians,
Jeez, they run into millions.

US Army, Second World War

Preface to *The Uncommercial Traveller* (1861)

Any animated description of a modern battle, any private soldier's letter published in the newspapers, any page of the records of the Victoria Cross, will show that in the ranks of the Army there exists under all disadvantages as fine a sense of duty as to be found in any station on earth. Who doubts that if we did our duty as faithfully as the soldier does his, this world would be a better place? There may be greater difficulties in our way than in the soldier's. Not disputed. But let us at least do our duty toward him.

Charles Dickens

On 13 May 1940, while German armies swept across the Meuse into France, Winston Churchill made his first speech as Prime Minister to the House of Commons:

I have nothing to offer but blood, toil, tears and sweat . . . You ask, What is our policy? I will say: It is to wage war, by sea, land and air, with all our might and with all the strength that God can give us: to wage war against a monstrous tyranny, never surpassed in the dark, lamentable catalogue of human crime. That is our policy. You ask, What is our aim? I can answer in one word: Victory – victory at all costs, victory in spite of all terror; victory, however long and hard the road may be; for without victory there is no survival.

Churchill's speech, House of Commons, 4 June 1940

Even though large tracts of Europe and many old and famous States have fallen or may fall into the grip of the Gestapo and all the odious apparatus of Nazi rule, we shall not flag or fail. We shall go on to the end. We shall fight in France, we shall fight in the seas and oceans, we shall fight with growing confidence and growing strength in the air; we shall defend our Island, no matter what the cost may be. We shall fight on the beaches, we shall fight on the landing-grounds, we shall fight in the fields and in the streets, we shall fight in the hills; we shall never surrender.

On 18 June Churchill again addressed the House of Commons. The speech was subsequently broadcast:

The whole fury and might of the enemy must very soon be turned on us. Hitler knows that he will have to break us in this Island or else lose the war. If we can stand up to him, all Europe may be free and the life of the world may move forward into broad, sunlit uplands. But if we fail, then the whole world, including the United States, including all that we have known and cared for, will sink into the abyss of a new Dark Age, made more sinister, and perhaps more protracted, by the lights of perverted science. Let us therefore brace ourselves to our duties, and so bear ourselves that, if the British Empire and its Commonwealth last for a thousand years, men will still say: 'This was their finest hour.'

Winston Churchill mobilized the English language and sent it into battle to steady his fellow countrymen and hearten the Europeans upon whom the long night of tyranny had descended.

Ed Murrow – U S newscaster

Battle of Crécy, 26 August 1346

You must know, that these kings, earls, barons and lords of France, did not advance in any regular order, but one after the other, or any way most pleasing to themselves. As soon as the king of France came in sight of the English, his blood began to boil, and he cried out to his marshals, 'Order the Genoese forward, and begin the battle, in the name of God and St Denis.' There were about fifteen thousand Genoese cross-bowmen; but they were quite fatigued, having marched on foot that day six leagues, completely armed, and with their cross-bows. They told the constable, they were not in a fit condition to do any great things that day in battle. The earl of Alençon, hearing this, said, 'This is what one gets by employing such scoundrels, who fall off when there is any need for them.' During this time a heavy rain fell, accompanied by thunder and a very terrible eclipse of the sun; and before this rain a great flight of crows hovered in the air over all the battalions, making a loud noise. Shortly afterwards it cleared up, and the sun shone very bright; but the Frenchmen had it in their faces, and the English in their backs. When the Genoese were somewhat in order, and approached the English, they set up a great shout, in order to frighten them; but they remained quite still, and did not seem to attend it. They then set up a second shout, and advanced a little forward; but the English never moved. They hooted a third time, advancing with their cross-bows presented, and began to shoot. The English archers then advanced one step forward, and shot their arrows with such force and quickness, that it seemed as if it snowed. When the Genoese felt these arrows, which pierced their arms, heads, and through their armour, some of them cut the strings of their cross-bows, others flung them on the ground, and all turned about and retreated quite discomfited. The French had a large body of men at arms on horseback, richly dressed, to support the Genoese. The king of France, seeing them thus fall back, cried out, 'Kill me those scoundrels; for they step up our road, without any reason.' You would then have seen the above-mentioned men at arms lay about them, killing all they could of these runaways.

Jean Froissart
Chronicles I.*cxxix*

The Sentinel's Story

After the Battle of Trafalgar the body of Lord Nelson was placed in a leaguer (large barrel) of brandy as the *Victory* sailed for Gibraltar.

On the night of 24 October, owing to a displacement of air from the corpse, the lid of the cask burst open and the body reappeared, resulting in a rumour that the Admiral had risen from the dead.

THREE days below Trafalgar
Walking the western swell,
Where in the Shoals of Peter
Many deep-seamen dwell,
Our ship, wearing the weather,
Taut as the travelling tree,
Now shook its hundred branches
On forests of the sea.

The Captain in his cabin
Slept in the walnut wood,
Jack Strop within his swinging bed,
The nipper where he could.
Some slept above and some below
The waving water-line,
But soundest slept the Admiral
Buried in brandy-wine.

fought like the devil, sit down and cry like a
wench. I am still in the *Royal Sovereign*, but the
Admiral [Collingwood] has left her, for she is like
a horse without a bridle, so he is in a frigate that he
may be here and there and everywhere, for he's as
cute as here and there one, and as bold as a lion, for
all he can cry! I saw his tears with my own eyes,
when the boat hailed and said my Lord was dead.
So no more at present from

Your dutiful Son,

Sam

Taken from *Christmas Crackers*
John Julius Norwich

In the midst of the conflict
Great Nelson undaunted,
Regarded nor balls nor the wave,
But order'd the grog
When the British tars wanted,
And told us what England expects from the brave!

John Nicolson

Anthem for Doomed Youth

What passing-bells for these who die as cattle?
Only the monstrous anger of the guns.
Only the stuttering rifles' rapid rattle
Can patter out their hasty orisons.
No mockeries now for them; no prayers nor bells,
Nor any voice of mourning save the choirs,–
The shrill, demented choirs of wailing shells;
And bugles calling for them from sad shires.

What candles may be held to speed them all?
Not in the hands of boys, but in their eyes
Shall shine the holy glimmers of good-byes.
The pallor of girls' brows shall be their pall;
Their flowers the tenderness of patient minds,
And each slow dusk a drawing-down of blinds.

Wilfred Owen

Lest We Forget

At the going down of the sun, and in the
morning,
we will remember them.

Laurence   Binyon

I Remember, I Remember

I remember, I remember,
The house where I was born,
The little window where the sun
Came peeping in at morn;
He never came a wink too soon,
Nor brought too long a day,
But now, I often wish the night
Had borne my breath away!

I remember, I remember,
The roses, red and white,
The violets, and the lily-cups,
Those flowers made of light!
The lilacs where the robin built,
And where my brother set
The laburnum on his birthday, –
The tree is living yet!

I remember, I remember,
Where I was used to swing,
And thought the air must rush as fresh
To swallows on the wing;
My spirit flew in feathers then,
That is so heavy now,
And summer pools could hardly cool
The fever on my brow!

I remember, I remember,
The fir trees dark and high;
I used to think their slender tops
Were close against the sky:
It was a childish ignorance,
But now 'tis little joy
To know I'm farther off from heaven
Than when I was a boy.

Thomas Hood

In Memorium (Easter 1915)

The flowers, left thick at night fall in the wood
This Eastertide, call into mind the men,
Now far from home, who, with their sweethearts, should
Have gathered them and will do never again.

Edward Thomas

Praising what is lost makes the
remembrance dear.

William Shakespeare

This Grumpy Old Man is Moved to Tears

There has been a funny four-part programme on BBC2 called *Grumpy Old Men* in which a group of what I would call young-middle-aged men (i.e., they are mostly my age) complain about the inadequacies of modern life in general and young people in particular.

The programme features rants from the likes of Bill Nighy, John Sessions, Arthur Smith, Will Self and Rick Wakeman. But the grumpy old man I particularly enjoy is Bob Geldof, whose bad-tempered take on the whole business of fatherhood clearly belies a devoted dad.

Last week, he made the point that, when he was at school, his father came to maybe one event in the whole of his school career, whereas Geldof has turned up to every nativity play, concert, assembly and drama in which his children have been even remotely involved.

He then launched into the sort of sweeping generalisation that makes the programme so enjoyable, by stating that all these productions have been "shite" and that everything that you have to go and see as a parent is terrible. I laughed a lot, as I am sure did many parents, with that guilty laughter of recognition.

But I had to swallow my laughter later. A school service and concert on Remembrance Sunday made me remember that when children perform it can be a lot more moving than adults.

The event was run along traditional lines but there was a particularly good section where they showed photographs taken on a school trip to the First World War cemeteries in Normandy. These simple images appeared on a big screen, accompanied by Elgar's *Nimrod* from *Enigma Variations*.

On one headstone a young soldier's age was recorded as 15, which is only a few years older than the children taking part, and well within their experience of siblings and friends. There were readings from First World War diaries and poems, and a chorus singing a bit of Pergolesi's *Stabat Mater*. There were the hymns *I Vow to thee my Country* and *Abide with Me*, accompanied by the school brass group. The Last Post was played by boys of exactly the type who, in a previous generation, would have been in France playing it at their friends' funerals.

I was, as usual on this day, choked up at the thought of how little my generation has been called upon to do, and how desperately I hoped that the same would be true of my son's. Oddly enough, what really tipped me over the edge was a choir of boys and girls singing *There'll be Blue Birds Over the White Cliffs of Dover*. Written by the American lyricist Nat Burton, who had never been to Dover and did not know what sort of birds flew there anyway, and set to schmaltzy music by Walter Kent, this sentimental pop song should have seemed flimsy and out of place. Yet context is everything, and the fact that this song was written in 1941 makes its melancholy optimism about victory immensely affecting.

Strangely, the last time I heard anyone singing this was Vera Lynn herself standing on the back of a lorry on Ditchling Beacon as part of the Queen's Silver Jubilee celebrations in 1977.

My uncle had just died and, feeling less than celebratory, my cousins and I walked up the beacon to see the fire that had been lit. We turned a corner in the dark to find her there, belting it out over the South

Downs. It was curiously comforting in the circumstances, and I have had a soft spot for it ever since.

This might explain my reaction but I think that I am going to have to make this Remembrance event an exception to Geldof's rule. It also made me question press reports suggesting that young people no longer connect with the events that are being remembered, and are not interested in their own history. I hope that this will prove to be an over-grumpy analysis of the situation.

Ian Hislop
Sunday Telegraph Review

Remember me when you do pray
That hope doth lead from day to day.

Anne Boleyn
From her own Book of Hours

For the Fallen (September 1914)

With proud thanksgiving, a mother for her children,
England mourns for her dead across the sea.
Flesh of her flesh they were, spirit of her spirit,
Fallen in the cause of the free.

Solemn the drums thrill: Death august and royal
Sings sorrow up into immortal spheres.
There is music in the midst of desolation
And a glory that shines upon our tears.

They went with songs to the battle, they were young,
Straight of limb, true of eye, steady and aglow.
They were staunch to the end against odds uncounted,
They fell with their faces to the foe.

They shall grow not old, as we that are left grow old:
Age shall not weary them, nor the years condemn.
At the going down of the sun and in the morning
We will remember them.

They mingle not with their laughing comrades again;
They sit no more at familiar tables of home;
They have no lot in our labour of the day-time;
They sleep beyond England's foam.

But where our desires are and our hopes profound,
Felt as a well-spring that is hidden from sight,
To the innermost heart of their own land they are known
As the stars are known to the Night;

As the stars that shall be bright when we are dust,
Moving in marches upon the heavenly plain,
As the stars that are starry in the time of our darkness,
To the end, to the end, they remain.

Laurence Binyon

In Flanders Fields

IN Flanders fields the poppies blow
Between the crosses, row on row
*   That mark our place; and in the sky*
*   The larks, still bravely singing, fly*
Scarce heard amid the guns below.

We are the Dead. Short days ago
We lived, felt dawn, saw sunset glow,
*   Loved and were loved, and now we lie*
*   In Flanders fields.*

Take up our quarrel with the foe:
To you from failing hands we throw
*   The torch; be yours to hold it high.*
*   If ye break faith with us who die*
We shall not sleep, though poppies grow
*   In Flanders fields.*

John McCrae

When you go home, tell them of us and say,
For your tomorrows we gave our today.

From Soldier, Rest!

Soldier, rest! Thy warfare o'er,
   Sleep the sleep that knows not breaking;
Dream of battled fields no more,
   Days of danger, nights of waking.
In our isle's enchanted hall,
   Hands unseen thy couch are strewing,
Fairy strains of music fall,
   Every sense in slumber dewing.
Soldier, rest! Thy warfare o'er,
Dream of fighting fields no more:
Sleep the sleep that knows not breaking,
Morn of toil, nor night of waking.

Sir Walter Scott

The Soldier

If I should die, think only this of me:
*   That there's some corner of a foreign field*
That is for ever England. There shall be
*   In that rich earth a richer dust concealed;*
A dust whom England bore, shaped, made aware,
*   Gave, once, her flowers to love, her ways to roam,*
A body of England's breathing English air,
Washed by the rivers, blest by suns of home.

And think, this heart, all evil shed away,
*   A pulse in the eternal mind, no less*
*   Gives somewhere back the thoughts by England given;*
Her sights and sounds; dreams happy as her day;
*   And laughter, learnt of friends; and gentleness,*
*   In hearts at peace, under an English heaven.*

Rupert Brooke

The Battle of Britain

For Johnny

Do not despair
For Johnny-head-in-air;
He sleeps as sound
As Johnny underground.

Fetch out no shroud
For Johnny-in-the-cloud;
And keep your tears
For him in after years.

Better by far
For Johnny-the-bright-star,
To keep your head,
And see his children fed.

John Pudney

Remembrance

You are not gone
While still I see
Your face in my thoughts and dreams
Your smile to stem the tears
You are not gone
While still I hear
Your voice in distant echoes
Your laugh to calm my fears
You are not gone
While still I feel
Your hand reaching out for mine
Your presence always there
You are not gone
While still I have
Your love to keep in my heart
And family joys to share
While still I have
The memory of you
You are not gone.

Marion Griffin

Remember

Remember me when I am gone away,
Gone far away into the silent land;
When you can no more hold me by the hand,
Nor I half turn to go, yet turning stay.
Remember me when no more day by day
You tell me of our future that you planned:
Only remember me; you understand
It will be late to counsel then or pray,
Yet if you should forget me for a while
And afterwards remember, do not grieve:
For if the darkness and corruption leave
A vestige of the thoughts that once I had,
Better by far you should forget and smile
Than that you should remember and be sad.

Christina Rossetti

English – the Universal Language

That great Englishman, Sir Winston Churchill, wrote of his early life: 'By being so long in the lowest form I gained an immense advantage over the cleverer boys. They all went on to learn Latin and Greek, and splendid things like that. But I was taught English. We were considered such dunces that we could learn *only* English. As I remained in the Third Form three times as long as anyone else, I had three times as much of it. I learned it thoroughly. Thus I got into my bones the essential structure of the ordinary British sentence which is a noble thing.'

The English

We could start by considering what the English have given the world.

And here is the first problem. For the greatest legacy the English have bequeathed the rest of humanity is their language. When an Icelander meets a Peruvian, each reaches for his English. Even in the Second World War, when the foundations were being laid for the Axis pact between Germany, Japan and Italy, Yosuke Matsuoka was negotiating for the Emperor in English. It is the medium of technology, science, travel and international politics. Three quarters of the world's mail is written in English, four fifths of all data stored on computers is in English and the language is used by two thirds of the world's scientists. It is the Malay of the world, easy to learn, very easy to speak badly; a little learning will take you quite a long way, which is why an estimated one quarter of the entire world population can speak the language to some degree. By the late 1990s, the British Council was predicting that at the turn of the millennium 1 billion (thousand million) people would be learning English.

Jeremy Paxman
The English

So now they have made our English tongue
    a gallimaufry or hodge podge of all other
    speeches.

Edmund Spenser

The first words spoken on the moon were English. Bled white by two world wars, unable to balance its economy and stagnating under constant Union rows, England no longer takes a leading role in the decisions of the world.

But in spite of all this it has left one great legacy – its language.

The Hong Kong *China Mail*

The Asterisk

A writer owned an asterisk,
And kept it in his den,
Where he wrote tales (which had large sales)
Of frail and erring men;
And always, when he reached the point
Where carping censors lurk,
He called upon the asterisk
To do his dirty work.

Anon

Sticklers and Pedants

In her hugely entertaining book on punctuation, *Eats, Shoots and Leaves*, Lynne Truss admits that there is little profit in asking for sympathy for 'sticklers'. 'We are not the easiest people to feel sorry for', she says. 'We refuse to patronise any shop with checkouts for "eight items or less", (because it should be "fewer"), and we got worked up after 9/11 not because of Osama bin-Laden but because people on the radio kept saying "enormity" when they meant "magnitude", and we really hate that . . . Sticklers never read a book without a pencil at hand, to correct the typographical errors. In short, we are unattractive know-all obsessives who get things out of proportion and are in continual peril of being disowned by our exasperated families.'

John Humphrys agrees, as this extract from his book *Lost For Words* confirms:

'Why do so many despise pedants? Probably because they are often people who know more than we do and are not afraid to say so. They can't win. If people know less than we do we call them ignorant; if they know more we call them pedants. Nor is it true that they are all in their twilight years with nothing better to do than search out nits to pick. Here's part of a letter I received following a *Sunday Times* article:

A preposition should never end a sentence. Ever. On pain of death. OK, maybe not on pain of death, but at least on pain of angry stares and a good deal of sulking . . . To me it's the verbal equivalent of two bits of polystyrene rubbing together; unbearable.

The letter was written by a seventeen-year-old A-level student. What was wonderful about it was her strength of feeling. As it happens, I agree with her about polystyrene but not about prepositions. Mostly it is better not to end sentences with one, but not always.'

Sir Winston Churchill once famously rebuked a civil servant who had had the temerity to correct one of the Great Man's speeches because it ended a sentence with a preposition. An angry Churchill returned it to the offender with this note scribbled on it, 'This is a practice, up with which I will not put!'

Bleviee it or not! You are not going to believe this one

Aoccdrnig to rscheearch at Cmabrigde Uinervtisy, it deosn't mttaer in what order the ltteers in a word are, the only iprmoetnt thing is that the frist and lsat ltter be at the rghit pclae.

The rset can be a total mses and you can still raed it wouthit a porbelm. This is bcuseae the huamn mind deos not raed ervey lteter by istlef, but the word as a wlohe.

Amzanig, huh?

Shakespeare and Churchill

Each in their different centuries, these two men have been the greatest exponents of the English language. In his erudite history of the English language, *The Adventure of English*, Melvyn Bragg notes:

> Over 400 years ago, Shakespeare had a vocabulary of at least twenty-one thousand different words; some have estimated that with the combination of words, this could have reached thirty thousand. Comparisons are entertaining; the King James Bible of 1611 had about ten thousand different words. The average educated man today, more than four hundred years on from Shakespeare, with the advantage of the hundreds of thousands of new words that have come in since his time, has a working vocabulary of less than half that of Shakespeare.

Commenting on Churchill in the *Daily Telegraph* in early 2005, Melvyn Bragg reminded us of Churchill's oratory and his modesty. When, some years after the conflict, Churchill was asked to comment on his pivotal role in the Second World War, he replied, 'The nation had the lion's heart, I had the luck to give the roar.'

'I think he was absolutely accurate when he said that,' says Bragg. 'The British people wanted a roar. They wanted the huge feeling that great language can give. They wanted it articulated that they were taking part in something immensely significant for the history of the world. We were tuppence ha'penny away from being occupied and Churchill met the need that this country had to be inspired for a great war, and an improbable victory. You could say that what Churchill brought to a unique situation was a lifetime of preparation.'

Rotten at classics, worse still at maths, Churchill had left Harrow School in 1893 with a prize for English the only exception in a singularly unimpressive academic career. He was nevertheless accepted into Sandhurst Military Academy, albeit only after his third attempt at passing the entrance exam, and was swiftly dispatched to India. 'When he got there,' says Bragg, 'he discovered a lot of very clever young men and realised that if he really wanted to get ahead in politics, he would have to educate himself.'

In the following six months, Churchill devoured twelve volumes of Macaulay, all 4,000 pages of Gibbon's *Decline and Fall*, Plato's *Republic* (in translation), Aristotle's *Politics* (ditto), Darwin's *On the Origin of Species*, Schoppenhauer on pessimism and Smith's *Wealth of Nations*. This feat of scholarship furnished Churchill with the immense vocabulary, thorough grasp of rhetoric, and gift for the memorable phrase that would later serve him so well as a statesman and eventually, in 1953, win him the Nobel Prize for Literature.

English Is a Crazy Language

Let's face it – English is a crazy language. There is no egg in eggplant nor ham in hamburger; neither apple nor pine in pineapple. English muffins weren't invented in England or French fries in France. Sweetmeats are candies while sweetbreads, which aren't sweet, are meat.

We take English for granted. But if we explore its paradoxes, we find that quicksand can work slowly, boxing rings are square and a guinea pig is neither from Guinea nor is it a pig.

And why is it that writers write but fingers don't fing, grocers don't groce and hammers don't ham? If the plural of tooth is teeth, why isn't the plural of booth beeth? One goose, two geese. So one loose tooth, two leese teeth? One index, two indices?

Doesn't it seem crazy that you can make amends but not an amend, that you comb through annals of history but not a single annal? If you have a bunch of odds and ends and get rid of all but one of them, what do you call it?

If teachers taught, why didn't preachers praught? If a vegetarian eats vegetables, what does a humanitarian eat? If you wrote a letter, perhaps you bote your tongue?

Sometimes I think all the English speakers should be committed to an asylum for the verbally insane. In what language do people recite at a play and play at a recital? Ship by truck and send cargo or a truck by ship? Have noses that run and feet that smell? Park on driveways and drive on parkways? Lift a thumb to thumb a lift? Table a plan in order to plan a table?

How can a slim chance and a fat chance be the same, while a wise man and wise guy are opposites? How can overlook and oversee be opposites, while quite a lot and quite a few are alike? How can a person be 'pretty ugly'?

How can the weather be hot as hell one day and cold as hell another. Have you noticed that we talk about certain things only when they are absent? Have you ever seen a horseful carriage or a strapful gown? Met a sung hero or experienced requited love? Have you ever run into someone who was combobulated, gruntled, ruly or peccable? And where are all those people who really are spring chickens or who would actually hurt a fly?

You have to marvel at the unique lunacy of a language in which your house can burn up as it burns down, in which you fill in a form by filling it out and in which an alarm clock goes off by going on. Why is 'crazy man' an insult, while to insert a comma and say 'crazy, man!' is a compliment (as when applauding a jazz performance).

English was invented by people, not computers, and it reflects the creativity of the human race (which, of course, isn't a race at all). That is why, when the stars are out, they are visible, but when the lights are out, they are invisible. And why, when I wind up my watch, I start it, but when I wind up this essay, I end it.

An Amusing Rant
Anon
Gleaned from the Internet

Language is the dress of thought.

Samuel Johnson

Hints on Pronunciation For Foreigners

I take it you already know
Of tough and bough and cough and dough?
Others may stumble, but not you
On hiccough, thorough, laugh and through?
Well done! And now you wish perhaps
To learn of these familiar traps?

Beware of heard, a dreadful word,
That looks like beard and sounds like bird,
And dead: it's said like bed, not bead,
For Goodness' sake, don't call it deed!
Watch out for meat and great and threat,
They rhyme with suite and straight and debt.

A moth is not a moth in mother
Nor both in bother, broth in brother,
And here is not a match for there,
Nor dear and fear for bear and pear,
And then there's does and rose and lose –
Just look them up: and goose and choose,

And cork and front and word and ward
And font and front and word and sword.
And do and go and thwart and cart –
Come, come, I've hardly made a start!
A dreadful language? Man Alive,
I'd mastered it when I was five!

Anon

Why English Is So Hard

We'll begin with a box, and the plural is boxes;
But the plural of ox should be oxen, not oxes.
Then one fowl is goose, but two are called geese;
Yet the plural of moose should never be meese.
You may find a lone mouse or a whole lot of mice,
But the plural of house is houses, not hice.
If the plural of man is always called men,
Why shouldn't the plural of pan be called pen?
The cow in the plural may be cows or kine,
But the plural of vow is vows, not vine.
And I speak of a foot, and you show me your feet,
But I give you a boot – would a pair be called beet?
If one is a tooth and a whole set are teeth,
Why shouldn't the plural of booth be called beeth?
If the singular is this, and the plural is these,
Should the plural of kiss be nicknamed kese?
Then one may be that, and three may be those,
Yet the plural of hat would never be hose;
We speak of a brother, and also of brethren,
But though we say mother, we never say methren.
The masculine pronouns are he, his, and him.
But imagine the feminine she, shis, and shim!
So our English, I think you will all agree,
Is the trickiest language you ever did see.

Anon

Gobbledegook

In March 2002 Simon Hoggart wrote an article in the *Guardian* about the modern concept of 'management' that produces convoluted English and gobbledegook. He cited the following job advertisement as an example of the obfuscation:

> 'This key role manages corporate planning and performance processes within a Best Value framework to drive business improvement. Operating at a strategic level, the successful applicant will be required to manage the Corporate planning function and performance review framework, including Best Value and developing key system processes . . .'

Hoggart went on to ask, 'Can you work out what the job involves, or what the organisation that placed the ad does? Of course not! In fact it is head of corporate planning for the Hertfordshire Police. No wonder you never see a copper on the beat these days – they're all "driving business improvement", whatever that may be.'

Word Counts

The Lord's Prayer contains 69 words

The Ten Commandments contain 297 words

The American Declaration of Independence contains 310 words

The European Union directive on exporting duck eggs contains 28,911 words!

Spell Check?

With computers doing all the checking, we can now all spell as well as we could do calculations before the pocket calculator!

Eye halve a spelling chequer
It came with my pea sea.
It plainly marques four my revue
Miss steaks eye kin knot sea.
Eye strike a key and type a word
And weight four it two say
Weather eye am wrong oar write
It shows me strait a weigh.

As soon as a mist ache is maid
It nose bee fore two long
And eye can put the error rite
Its rare lea ever wrong.

Eye have run this poem threw it
I am shore your pleased two no
Its letter perfect awl the weigh
My chequer tolled me sew.

Sauce uknown

O Wud Some Pow'r the
Giftie Gie Us
To See Oursels As Others
See Us!

An Englishman, even if he is alone,

Forms an orderly queue of one.

George Mikes –

Hungarian-born British humorist

Notes From a Small Island

We drove home over the tops, a winding, 6-mile drive of unutterable loveliness, up on to the *Wuthering Heights*-like expanses around Kirkby Fell, with boundless views of Northern glory, and then began the descent into the serene, cupped majesty of Malhamdale, the little lost world that had been my home for seven years. Halfway down, I had my wife stop the car by a field gate. My favourite view in the world is there, and I got out to have a look. You can see almost the whole of Malhamdale; sheltered and snug beneath steep, imposing hills, with its arrow-straight drystone walls climbing up impossibly ambitious slopes, its clustered hamlets, its wonderful little two-room schoolhouse, the old church with its sycamores and tumbling tombstones, the roof of my local pub, and in the centre of it all, obscured by trees, our old stone house, which itself is far older than my native land.

It looked so peaceful and wonderful that I could almost have cried, and yet it was only a tiny part of this small, enchanted island. Suddenly, in the space of a moment, I realised what it was that I loved about Britain – which is to say, all of it. Every last bit of it, good and bad – Marmite, village fêtes, country lanes, people saying 'mustn't grumble' and 'I'm terribly sorry but', people apologising to *me* when I conk them with a careless elbow, milk in bottles, beans on toast, haymaking in June, stinging nettles, seaside piers, Ordnance Survey maps, crumpets, hot-water bottles as a necessity, drizzly Sundays – every bit of it.

What a wondrous place this was – crazy as f**k, of course, but adorable to the tiniest degree. What other country, after all, could possibly have come up with place names like Tooting Bec and Farleigh Wallop, or a game like cricket that goes on for three days and never seems to start? Who else would think it not the least odd to make their judges wear little mops on their heads, compel the Speaker of the House of Commons to sit on something called the Woolsack, or take pride in a military hero whose dying wish was to be kissed by a fellow named Hardy? ... What other nation in the world could possibly have given us William Shakespeare, pork pies, Christopher Wren, Windsor Great Park, the Open University, *Gardeners' Question Time*, and the chocolate digestive biscuit? None, of course.

Bill Bryson

From The White Cliffs

I have loved England, dearly and deeply,
Since the first morning, shining and pure,
The white cliffs of Dover I saw rising steeply
Out of the sea that once made her secure.

I had no thought then of husband or lover,
I was a traveller, the guest of a week;
Yet when they pointed 'the white cliffs of Dover',
Startled I found there were tears on my cheek.

I have loved England, and still as a stranger,
Here is my home and I still am alone.
Now in her hour of trial and danger,
Only the English are really her own.

And were they not English, our forefathers, never more
English than when they shook the dust of her sod
From their feet for ever, angrily seeking a shore
Where in his own way a man might worship his God.
Never more English than when they dared to be
Rebels against her – that stern intractable sense
Of that which no man can stomach and still be free,
Writing: 'When in the course of human events ...'
Writing it out so all the world could see
Whence come the powers of all just governments.
The tree of Liberty grew and changed and spread,
But the seed was English.

I am American bred,
I have seen much to hate here – much to forgive,
But in a world where England is finished and dead,
I do not wish to live.

Alice Duer Miller

And get me to England once again
For England's the one land I know
Where men with Splendid Hearts may go.

Rupert Brooke

Happy is England! I could be content
To see no other verdure than its own.

John Keats

The noblest prospect which a Scotsman ever sees,
is the high road that leads him to England.

Samuel Johnson

As Others See Us

There is nothing so bad or so good that you will not find Englishmen doing it; but you will never find an Englishman in the wrong. He does everything on principle. He fights you on patriotic principles; he robs you on business principles; he enslaves you on imperial principles.

George Bernard Shaw, *The Man of Destiny*

The English have no respect for their language, and will not teach their children to speak it ... It is impossible for an Englishman to open his mouth, without making some other Englishman despise him.

George Bernard Shaw, *Pygmalion*

What Englishman will give his mind to politics as long as he can afford to keep a motor car?

George Bernard Shaw, *The Apple Cart*

We do not regard Englishmen as foreigners. We look on them only as rather mad Norwegians.

Halvard Lange – Norwegian historian and politician

On the Continent people have good food; in England people have good table manners.

George Mikes – Hungarian-born British humorist

Continental people have sex lives; the English have hot-water bottles.

George Mikes

The English are a nation of shopkeepers.

Napoleon

The English are as brave as lions, they are splendid sepoys, and very near equal to us.

A Ghurka soldier after the Battle of Bhurtpore, 1827

England is the only country in the world where the food is more dangerous than sex.

Jackie Mason – U S comedian

If an Englishman gets run down by a truck, he apologises to the truck.

Jackie Mason

English life, while very pleasant, is rather bland. I expected kindness and gentility and I found it, but there is such a thing as too much couth.

S J Perelman – U S humorist

England is nothing but the last ward of the European madhouse, and quite possibly it will prove to be the ward of particularly violent cases.

Leon Trotsky

Englishmen are babes in philosophy and so prefer faction-fighting to the labour of its unfamiliar thought.

W B Yeats – Irish poet and dramatist

You know what the Englishman's idea of compromise is? He says, Some people say there is a God. Some people say there is no God. The truth probably lies somewhere between these two statements.

W B Yeats

England Expects

Let us pause to consider the English.

*Who when they pause to consider themselves they get all
reticently thrilled and tinglish,*

Because every Englishman is convinced of one thing, viz.:

*That to be an Englishman is to belong to the most exclusive
club there is:*

*A club to which benighted bounders of Frenchmen and
Germans and Italians et cetera cannot even aspire to
belong,*

*Because they don't even speak English, and the Americans
are worst of all because they speak it wrong.*

*Englishmen are distinguished by their traditions and
ceremonials,*

*And also by their affection for their colonies and their
contempt for their colonials.*

*When foreigners ponder world affairs, why sometimes by
doubts they are smitten,*

*But Englishmen know instinctively that what the world
needs most is whatever is best for Great Britain.*

*They have a splendid navy and they conscientiously admire
it,*

*And every English schoolboy knows that John Paul Jones
was only an unfair American pirate.*

English people disclaim sparkle and verve,

But speak without reservations of their Anglo-Saxon reserve.

*After listening to little groups of English ladies and
gentlemen at cocktail parties and in hotels and Pullmans,
of defining Anglo-Saxon reserve I despair,*

But I think it consists of assuming that nobody else is there,

*And I shudder to think where Anglo-Saxon reserve ends
when I consider where it begins,*

Which is in a few high-pitched statements of what one's

income is and just what foods give one a rash and
whether one and one's husband or wife sleep in a double
bed or twins.
All good young Englishmen go to Oxford or Cambridge and
they all write and publish books before their graduation,
And I often wondered how they did it until I realized that
they have to do it because their genteel accents are so
developed that they can no longer understand each
other's spoken words so the written word is their only
means of intercommunication.
England is the last home of the aristocracy, and the art
of protecting the aristocracy from the encroachments of
commerce has been raised to quite an art,
Because in America a rich butter-and-egg man is only a rich
butter-and-egg man or at most an honorary LL.D of some
hungry university, but in England why before he knows
it he is Sir Benjamin Buttery, Bart.
Anyhow, I think the English people are sweet,
And we might as well get used to them because when they
slip and fall they always land on their own or somebody
else's feet.

Ogden Nash

An Englishman thinks he is moral when he is only
uncomfortable.

George Bernard Shaw

Very English
Institutions –
the Nation, They Serve

Institution /-tū'shən / n the act of instituting or establishing; that which is instituted or established; foundation; established order; enactment; a society or organisation established for some object, *esp* cultural, charitable or beneficent, or the building housing it; a custom or usage, *esp* one familiar or characteristic; the act by which a bishop commits a cure of souls to a priest; appointment of an heir; a system of principles or rules *(obs)*; that which institutes or instructs *(obs)*.

The Church of England

The Church of England plays a vital role in the life of the nation, proclaiming the Christian gospel in word and actions and providing services of Christian worship and praise. Its network of parishes covers the country, bringing a vital Christian dimension to the nation as well as strengthening community life in numerous urban, suburban and rural settings. Its cathedrals are centres of spirituality and service.

The Church of England has more than 27,000 ministers, less than half of whom are paid clergy. The balance is made up of licensed readers, non-stipendary ministers, active retired clergy and 1,100 chaplains in colleges, universities, hospitals, schools, prisons and the armed forces.

It is an ancient church with its roots going back to 597 when Pope Gregory the Great sent a mission led by St Augustine of Canterbury. The mission landed in Kent and began the work of converting the pagan peoples. What eventually became known as the English Church was the result of a combination of three streams of Christianity, the Roman tradition of St Augustine and his successors, the remnants of the old Romano-British church and the Celtic tradition coming down from Scotland and associated with people such as St Aidan and St Cuthbert.

These three streams came together as a result of increasing mutual contact and a number of local synods, of which the Synod of Whitby in 664 has traditionally been seen as the most important. With two Archbishops of Canterbury and York, the Church of England was part of the Western church and, until the Reformation, acknowledged the authority of the Pope. At the

Reformation the Western Church divided between those who continued to accept Papal authority and the various Protestant churches that repudiated it. The Church of England broke with Rome – the catalyst for this decision was the refusal of the Pope to annul the marriage of Henry VIII and Catherine of Aragon.

In the 17th century continuing tensions within the Church over theological and liturgical issues were among the factors that led to the English Civil War. The Church was associated with the losing Royalist side and during the period of the Commonwealth from 1649 to 1660 its bishops were abolished and the Book of Common Prayer was banned. With the restoration of the monarchy in 1660, this situation was reversed and in 1662 those clergy who could not accept this decision were forced to leave their posts. These dissenting clergy and their congregations were then persecuted until 1689 when the Toleration Act gave legal existence to those Protestant groups outside the Church of England who accepted the doctrine of the Trinity.

The settlement of 1689 has remained the basis of the constitutional position of the Church of England ever since. As well as being the established Church of England, the Church of England has also become the mother church of the Anglican Communion, a group of separate churches that are in communion with the Archbishop of Canterbury, and for whom he is the focus of unity.

From the Bishop of London

Although the Church of England is the established church, there is all the difference in the world between a state church and the establishment of the Church of England. In some ways the English Church is the most disestablished major church in Europe, lacking the support for the ecclesiastical heritage that even the French government provides. The crucial statement about the identity of the Church declares that the Church of England is part of the One Holy Catholic and Apostolic Church, worshipping the one true God, Father, Son and Holy Spirit. It professes the faith uniquely revealed in the Holy Scriptures and set forth in the Catholic creeds, which faith the church is called upon to proclaim afresh in each generation. Led by the Holy Spirit, it has borne witness to the Christian truth in its historic formularies, the XXXIX Articles of religion, the Book of Common Prayer and the Ordering of Bishops, Priests and Deacons. Every priest and bishop at their ordination or when entering into new work must declare their loyalty to this inheritance of faith as their inspiration and guidance under God in bringing the grace and truth of Christ to this generation.

The Rt. Revd. & Rt. Hon. Richard Chartres D D, F S A

The Prayer Book Society

The Prayer Book Society was founded in 1972 to protect the Book of Common Prayer (BCP), which a number of people feared was threatened by the new Alternative Service Book (ASB). Although they failed to stop the ASB (which came into use in 1980), they were successful in keeping the Prayer Book as 'a doctrinal standard'.

The BCP is often referred to as '1662' – the date of the last official revision – but its origins go back much further. It is to Archbishop Cranmer that we owe the beauty of the language that pervades the 1662 BCP. Cranmer exploited the opportunity provided by Henry VIII's break from Rome and the subsequent reform of the Church of England to translate the Prayer Book into English and he included new material as well as keeping much of the old traditional content.

By the 1950s, influential members of the Church of England felt that the BCP was no longer understood by many worshippers and they sought to introduce new forms of service to attract a new congregation. Fearful that the traditional Prayer Book would be abandoned in favour of the new 'light-weight' services, a group of busy people, clergy and laymen, formed the Prayer Book Society to defend the tried and tested traditional forms of service. Had it not been for the Prayer Book Society, it is very likely that there would be no traditional Prayer Book services in England now.

John Wesley wrote: 'I believe there is no liturgy in the world, either in ancient or modern language, which breathes more of a solid, scriptural, rational piety than the Common Prayer of the Church of England.'

That is what the Prayer Book Society believes and seeks to defend.

From the Bishop of London

The Prayer Book system embodies the ethos of this Church, which was founded on Scripture, interpreted by tradition, which is not only articulated by the Catholic creeds [which are perhaps more commonly used in the Prayer Book liturgies than in any other liturgical regimes], but which is also expressed by the spirit-filled continuity of life in the church and the ways in which we have sought together to respond to the demands of successive generations.

We are heirs of Shakespeare, not Racine, and we distrust ideological abstractions and that is why the Prayer Book is so important as an organic development of the historic liturgy of the church reformed in the light of the revelation in Holy Scripture!

The Prayer Book offers a simple and moderate system for a whole life, from baptism to last rites, and seeks in its rubrics and ceremonies to embrace the whole person and not merely the cerebellum.

The influence of the Prayer Book system, its language and the dispositions which it inculcates upon many generations, has played a major role in instilling in English culture the virtues of restraint and balance through a reading of the whole of scripture which has offered English people access to the conversation between God and his people in time and the possibility of seeing our own stories in the light of the story of Jesus Christ.

The Rt. Revd. & Rt. Hon. Richard Chartres D D, F S A

English Heritage

English Heritage was set up by Act of Parliament in 1984 to promote the enjoyment of properties in its care, to protect England's spectacular historic environment and also to ensure that its glories are researched and understood. The organisation carries out these roles by advising the Government on what should be protected, giving technical conservation advice, supporting archaeology and recording the sites, monuments, landscapes and places that make up the full historic panoply. English Heritage recognises that understanding of the past is rooted in knowledge. Its team of professional and technical staff are the standard-setters for all aspects of research into the historic environment. These standards are communicated through academic publishing, supporting research in universities, running and funding courses, and publishing policies and guidelines.

The English Heritage public archive, the National Monuments Record Centre in Swindon, holds more than 10 million items within its collections. It has its own archaeological laboratory, which does pioneering research in areas such as scientific dating methods, geophysics and the study of environmental remains. English Heritage directly manages more than 400 important historic sites, telling visitors about them, holding events in them and using them for education, leisure and enjoyment. Operating the Blue Plaque scheme is an important function and it is now being extended beyond London (which already has more than 800 plaques), to several other English cities.

In addition to designating battlefields and parks and gardens of special interest, English Heritage gives grants for the upkeep of churches and cathedrals.

The Queen's English Society

The Queen's English Society (QES) was founded in 1972 by Joe Clifton, an Oxford graduate and schoolteacher. A letter sent to his local newspaper deploring the current decline in standards of English had resulted in so many sympathetic letters from readers that he was encouraged to form a group to try to do something about the problem. More than thirty years later, the Society is considered an authority on good English and is regularly consulted by the media whenever the subject of standards in English is raised.

The objects of the Society are to promote the maintenance, knowledge, development and appreciation of the English language, as used both colloquially and in literature – to advise on its correct usage, and to discourage the intrusion of anything detrimental.

The QES is also very concerned about the education of children. Consequently, when it became evident that schools were no longer teaching English as well as it used to be taught, the QES delivered, in 1998, a petition to the Secretary of State for Education, urging him to 'introduce the compulsory study of formal grammar, including parsing and sentence analysis, into the school curriculum'.

The Society's quarterly journal, *Quest*, includes articles and letters from members plus details of current activities, book reviews and poems. The Society believes that the commitment to standards does not preclude the possibility of grammatical change; nor does it mean, however, that the 'living language' should be thoughtlessly celebrated for its own sake. The English language enables a sizeable portion of the world to consider and communicate the most sophisticated of abstract ideas, as well as the most complicated realities. We abuse it to our disadvantage.

The Plain English Campaign

It would be hard to overstate the effect the Plain English Campaign has had on clear communication in both the public and private sectors since its foundation in 1979, and it owes its present highly respected reputation to the zeal and determination of one woman – Christine Mayer. As with so many of her peers in postwar Britain, young Christine was deprived of a good education and was only rescued from a life of difficulty when her first employer, Henry Deverall, recognised her potential and paid for her to go to night school in Tuebrook, Liverpool.

By 1971 Christine, married with four children, realised that even her well-educated friends struggled to understand official information, and in particular had trouble with welfare benefit forms. She started a one-woman campaign to persuade the authorities to communicate in clear, comprehensive English. In 1979, dissatisfied with the rate of progress, she decided to launch a national campaign to force the Government and big business into action – and where better to launch it than in Parliament Square? With her daughter and some friends, she set up a table opposite the Houses of Parliament and set about shredding hundreds of official documents. Within minutes the police arrived to discover the source of the commotion. Surrounded by TV, radio and newspaper reporters, a police officer read out a 100-word sentence from the 1839 Metropolitan Police Act, full of archaic legalese. Christine asked, 'Does that gobbledegook mean we have to go?' The police officer had made Christine's point as forcibly as the shredding itself; the Plain English Campaign was on its way.

Today the Campaign is international and has a staff of 35, providing services to businesses large and small, and advises government departments and local authorities on all aspects of communication. It runs training courses, and offers the coveted 'Crystal Mark' to those organisations whose literature is clear and unambiguous.

And all because Christine Mayer (now the proud possessor of a well-deserved OBE) had a vision and the determination to see it come to life.

This England

At first glance, England's foremost patriotic magazine may seem an unlikely candidate for a section on English institutions, but its hundreds of thousands of loyal readers have no doubt that *This England* is, indeed, a very English institution.

This England is the brainchild of Roy Faiers who, as a young man, built a very successful career as a freelance journalist and went on to launch *Lincolnshire Life*, a general interest magazine about the county of his birth. This led to similar journals for other counties, and in 1968 he was inspired to start *This England*. Thirty-seven years later, the magazine has an impressive world readership of about two million for each quarterly issue.

The format has changed very little over the years. Beautiful photographs of idyllic English scenes accompany appropriate poems. The country's churches and cathedrals are regularly featured as part of the nation's heritage. Readers' letters include a regular section of requests for words of half-forgotten songs or poems – requests that are invariably answered by a knowledge-able readership in a subsequent issue.

In the early years, the historian Sir Arthur Bryant, the novelist R F Delderfield and the country author and poet J H B Peel were regular contributors, as was Patience Strong, whose poems still grace the back cover of every issue. Articles on country matters, historical events and stories of our heroes sit alongside features of the stars of yesterday and write-ups of our beautiful cities. Indeed, anything that typifies the traditional English way of life will be covered at some point. One of Roy Faiers's schoolfriends was Colin Carr, who became a first-rate artist, and his whimsical illustrations delighted readers for more than 30 years until his death in 2002.

Although non-party political, *This England*'s fiercely patriotic editorial policy has caused it to campaign vigorously against moves that adversely affect England and which, if allowed to go unchecked, could lead to the destruction of our Englishness. The first, in 1974, was a campaign to preserve our ancient shires and this was followed in 1978 by a campaign to prevent compulsory metrication. The magazine's Imperial Charter attracted more than 100,000 signatures. Since 1990, concerned at the threat to our sovereignty from the European Union, *This England* has conducted a vigorous opposition under the slogan 'Don't Let Europe Rule Britannia' – a campaign that has the full backing of its enthusiastic readership.

The Treasure Houses of England

The Treasure Houses of England group consists of ten of the largest independent historic properties in England. Eight of the houses are still lived in and run by the families that built them, while Leeds Castle is owned by a charitable foundation and Warwick Castle is now part of the Tussaud's Group.

Some of the houses have been open to visitors for more than two centuries. Collectively, they now attract more than 750,000 visitors each year, and, it is estimated, have received more than 121 million visitors in the postwar period. Four of the properties – Warwick Castle, Leeds Castle, Blenheim Palace and Chatsworth – are the most visited historic houses in the UK. All ten are outstanding examples of England's heritage, often spoken of as the 'jewels in the crown', by virtue of the quality of the collections, architecture, landscape or historical association.

With a slightly different membership, the Group was established more than 25 years ago with two principle objectives. First, its combined influence allows the consortium to take advantage of marketing and promotional opportunities that would not necessarily be available to individual properties. Second, it provides a confidential, and much used, forum within which owners and managers can discuss all matters of mutual interest.

Arundel Castle	Beaulieu	Blenheim Palace
Castle Howard	Chatsworth	Harewood
Leeds Castle	Warwick Castle	Wilton House
Woburn Abbey		

The English Folk Dance and Song Society

The English Folk Dance and Song Society (EFDSS) is recognised as England's national repository for folk arts materials. Since its inception it has evolved into an outstanding multi-media collection with the opening of Cecil Sharp House in 1930. However, its roots go much deeper . . .

Cecil Sharp (1859–1924), a music teacher from south London, was the most prolific folk music and dance collector of the 20th century. When he died his personal library was bequeathed to the EFDSS, thereby forming the Cecil Sharp Library and the nucleus of the library and archive that exists today. When Ralph Vaughan Williams (who was President of the EFDSS) died in 1958 and left his papers to the Society, the Cecil Sharp Library was renamed the Vaughan Williams Memorial Library in honour of the great composer.

Today the Library houses more than 20,000 items of literature, 10,000 sound recordings, 20,000 photographs and more than 500 tons of periodicals – all this in addition to a number of complete collections such as the BBC folk music archive and the audio and visual collection of Percy Grainger.

The Royal Botanic Gardens, Kew

The Royal Botanic Gardens at Kew attracts more than one million visitors a year to its historic landscape, its famous greenhouses, and its great living collection of more than 35,000 plant species from all over the world. For nearly 250 years Kew Gardens has been part of English history. Today it is one of the world's leading botanic gardens, combining wide-ranging plant sciences with horticulture and education, together directed towards an understanding of the world's plants and their place in the global ecosystem and economy.

When Frederick, Prince of Wales, died in 1751, his widow, Princess Augusta, began developing the garden in her Kew home, the White House, under the guidance of the 3rd Earl of Bute. In 1757 she appointed William Chambers to relandscape the grounds and several of his buildings, including the Orangery and the Pagoda, can still be seen today. The year 1759 saw the foundation of the gardens and the beginning of the scientific era at Kew. Princess Augusta's son, George III, commissioned Capability Brown to refashion the adjacent royal estate of Richmond Lodge and in 1772 the two estates were united.

Under the guidance of Sir Joseph Banks, from 1772 until his death in 1820, Kew steadily acquired an increasing international horticultural reputation and plant exploration was encouraged, resulting in about 7,000 new species being introduced into England during the reign of George III. From the appointment, in 1841, of Kew's first official Director, Sir William Hooker, and under his eminent successors, the Gardens have gone from strength to strength.

Kew is a primary international centre for the classification, identification and naming of plants and fungi, as well as for other fundamental botanical research, in support of which it maintains vast global reference collections (which include 7,500,000 dried specimens), one of the world's largest botanical libraries, and a collection of cryopreserved seeds. Kew's mission is 'To enable better management of the earth's environment by increasing knowledge and understanding of the plant and fungal kingdoms – the basis of life on earth'.

Kew Gardens is now a UNESCO World Heritage Site.

The English Poetry and Song Society

The English Poetry and Song Society (EPSS) exists to promote the public performance, publication and recording of English art songs.

The Society was founded in 1983 by poet and amateur musician Alfred Warren, who was enthused after hearing a radio broadcast of English songs by John Carol Case. The first half of the 20th century was a golden age for English art song and produced a vast repertoire of glorious songs, by all the best British composers, which has become sadly neglected. Twice a year the EPSS publishes a newsletter with sample songs and song-lists by living composers, and new poetry, as well as running competitions for composers. Concerts and recitals are also held, often as part of literary festivals. The organisation caters for both professional and amateur performers.

CAMRA – Campaign for Real Ale

English Ale has been the nation's tipple for centuries and has regularly featured in the literature of the country, most notably in G K Chesterton's poem 'The Englishman':

St George, he was for England
And before he killed the Dragon,
He drank a pint of English Ale
Out of an English flagon.

Well, English ale may not often be served in flagons these days, but the pint is still as popular as ever, and its quality is jealously guarded, and its benefits promoted, by the Campaign for Real Ale (CAMRA).

Founded in 1971, CAMRA, with more than 75,000 members, claims to be the largest single-issue consumer group in the UK. It was formed to halt the decline in good-quality beer that was being replaced by keg beer brands. Its aims are to promote and protect consumer rights, to promote quality, choice and value for money and to support the public house as a focus of community life. CAMRA campaigns for greater appreciation of traditional beers, ciders and perries as part of England's heritage and culture and seeks to promote and preserve full-flavoured and distinctive beers and good pubs.

One of the organisation's early successes was to persuade brewers to state the strength of their beers. Today there are more than 630 beers in production and the number of pubs that offer real ale exceeds 4,500. St George would be pleased.

English Wine Producers

English Wine Producers (EWP) is the marketing arm of the English wine industry. Mention English wines to a Continental winemaker and a few years ago you would have been treated to a supercilious smirk, but not today. Once considered to be the hobby of an eccentric few, it is now a widely respected and flourishing industry. Critics are surprised to learn that vines in England pre-date the Roman invasion. From *The Oxford Companion to Wine*, we learn that Glastonbury Abbey was granted a charter for a vineyard in AD 955 and that the high point of English winemaking occurred in the 12th and 13th centuries, coinciding with a period of warm climate change. Archaeologists are regularly finding evidence of commercial winemaking as far back as Roman times.

EWP represents members who, between them, account for more than 75 per cent of the country's production.

Currently, England boasts more than 320 vineyards and more than 100 wineries. Most of these are in the South East, though vineyards can be found as far west as Cornwall and as far north as Yorkshire. They vary in size, from just a few acres to the largest (Denbies Wine Estate) at 265 acres. Between them, they produce an average of 1.8 million bottles (mostly white wine) each year.

England is fast acquiring a reputation for sparkling wines that are made with the same grape varieties and same methods as Champagne. The South East has a great advantage in that the soil of the South Downs is very similar to that in Champagne country.

The English wine industry has shaken off its 'hobby' image and is prospering, but sadly for this book, the proudly named St George's vineyard has not survived into the 21st century.

Acknowledgements

This book would have been much the poorer but for the help received from many quarters. At the outset, Peter Barkworth, Michele Brown and W F 'Bill' Deedes gave me sound advice, which I have been pleased to take. I am also grateful to The Rt Revd and Rt Hon Richard Chartres D D, F S A, Anthony Cooney, Daphne Fido, Stephen Garnett, John Mitchell, Michael Plumbe, Martin Sands, Simon Seligman and Julia Trustram Eve for their valuable contributions. The splendid staff at the Poetry Library have also been enormously helpful and their assistance has been invaluable.

I am immensely indebted to Graham Byfield for generously providing the artwork for the cover and for allowing me to impose on him while he was embroiled in his latest opus, *An Oxford Sketchbook*. I am grateful, too, to Air Vice-Marshall 'Larry' Lamb, President, and Roger Chalfont, Chairman, of the St George's Day Club for their enthusiastic support.

Last, but certainly not least, my thanks to the good folk at Robson Books and in particular to Jane Donovan, my editor, who has steered me, patiently and skilfully, through the arcane processes of putting a book together, and to Helen Ponting and Melanie Letts, who have been never less than helpful at all times. But primarily my thanks must go to Jeremy Robson for having faith in the project and for his constructive comments and encouragement throughout.

Gerry Hanson

Useful addresses

CAMRA
230 Hatfield Road
St Albans
Hertfordshire AL1 4LW
Tel: 01727 867201

The Church of England
Church House
Great Smith Street
London SW1P 3NZ
Tel: 020 7898 1000

The English Folk Dance and
Song Society
Cecil Sharp House
2 Regent's Park Road
London NW1 7AY
Tel: 020 7485 2206

English Heritage
23 Savile Row
London W1S 2ET
Tel: 020 7973 3000

The English Poetry and Song
Society
76 Lower Oldfield Park
Bath
Somerset BA2 3HP
Tel: 01225 313531

English Wine Producers
PO Box 5729
Market Harborough
Leicestershire LE16 8WX
Tel: 01536 772264

The Plain English Campaign
PO Box 3
New Mills
High Peak SK22 4QP
Tel: 01663 744409

The Prayer Book Society
The Studio
Copyhold Farm
Goring Heath
Oxon RG8 7RT
Tel: 0118 984 2582

The Queen's English Society
The Clergy House
Hide Place
London SW1P 4NJ
Tel: 020 7630 1819

The Royal Botanic Gardens
Kew, Richmond
Surrey TW9 3AB
Tel: 020 8332 5655
(information)/020 8332 5000
(switchboard)

The Royal Society of St George
127 Sandgate Road
Folkestone
Kent CT20 2BH
Tel: 01303 241795

The St George's Day Club
112 Waverley Road
Harrow
Middlesex HA2 9RE
Tel: 020 8868 7562

This England Magazine
Alma House
73 Rodney Road
Cheltenham
Gloucestershire GL50 1HT
Tel: 01242 537900

Sources

The Compiler's thanks to the following for permission to publish certain copyright material:

Dr Dannie Abse for 'Not Addlestrop' from *New & Collected Poems* (Hutchinson).

André Deutsch for 'England Expects' by Ogden Nash from *Candy is Dandy: The Best of Ogden Nash* (André Deutsch).

Sheila Arnoldi for 'On the Rose'.

Melvyn Bragg for an extract from *The Adventure of English* (Sceptre).

Chatsworth Library and Chatsworth Trust for the illustration of Queen Victoria arriving at Chatsworth, page 95.

Alan Coren for 'A Credit to Oxford' (© Alan Coren), from *The Cricklewood Tapestry* (Robson Books).

Curtis Brown Group Ltd, on behalf of the trustees of the Pooh Properties for 'Buckingham Palace' by A A Milne from *When We Were Very Young*. Also on behalf of Winston S Churchill for extracts from Sir Winston Churchill's speeches and *My Early Life* © Winston S Churchill.

David Higham Associates for 'The Sentinel's Story' by Charles Causley from *Collected Poems* (Macmillan). Also for an extract from *Eats, Shoots and Leaves* by Lynne Truss (Profile Books).

Francis Day & Hunter Ltd for 'I Leave my Heart in an English Garden' by Christopher Hassall.

Chris de Burgh and Hornall Brothers Music Ltd for 'Rose of England' by Chris de Burgh.

Marion Griffin for 'Remembrance'.

Ian Hislop and *The Sunday Telegraph* for 'This Grumpy Old Man'.

John Humphrys for an extract from *Lost for Words*, Hodder & Stoughton.

James Delingpole and *The Times* for 'We English are so Great'.

International Music Publications for 'We'll Gather Lilacs' by Ivor Novello and for 'Rose of England' by Ivor Novello and Christopher Hassall, and for 'Song of Patriotic Prejudice' and 'Song of the Weather' by Michael Flanders (© The Estates of Michael Flanders and Donald Swann). Also for 'O Peaceful England' and 'The English Rose' from Merrie England by Edward German and Basil Hood.

John Murray Publishers for 'In Westminster Abbey' by John Betjeman from *Collected Poems*.

Methuen Publishing for 'The Stately Homes of England' and 'Lie in the Dark and Listen' by Noël Coward from *Collected Verse* (Methuen Publishing Ltd).

Sir John Mortimer for the extract from *My Oxford*, © Advanpress Ltd, Robson Books.

Peter Newbolt for 'Vitai Lampada' and 'Drake's Drum' by Sir Henry Newbolt from *Selected Poems of Henry Newbolt* (Hodder & Stoughton, 1982).

Jeremy Paxman for extracts from The English (Michael Joseph, 1998).

Pollinger Ltd and the Estate of Alice Duer Miller for the extract from her poem, 'The White Cliffs' (© Alice Duer Miller).

Richard, Earl of Bradford, for extracts from *Porter's English Cookery Bible, Ancient and Modern* (Robson Books, 2004).

Shapiro, Bernstein & Co Inc for 'There'll be Bluebirds Over the White Cliffs of Dover' by Nat Burton and Walter Kent.

Sheil Land Associates for 'It's Almost Tomorrow' by Joyce Grenfell from *Turn Back the Clock* (Sceptre, © Joyce Grenfell).

The Society of Authors on behalf of the Estate of John Masefield for 'Sea Fever' and on behalf of the Estate of Laurence Binyon for 'For the Fallen' (September 1914).

Dr David Starkey and the *Daily Telegraph* for 'The Country that Dare Not Speak its Name'.

This England magazine for the illustration of Alma House, Cheltenham, page 213.

Transworld Publishers for an extract from *Notes from a Small Island* by Bill Bryson (© Black Swan).

A P Watt Ltd, on behalf of the National Trust, for 'The Glory of the Garden' and extracts from 'The Return' and 'The English Flag' by Rudyard Kipling (from the Definitive edition of Kipling verse, Hodder & Stoughton). Also on behalf of The Royal Literary Fund for three poems by G K Chesterton from *Other Men's Flowers* (Jonathan Cape, 1996).